AF278713

God Loves Abused Women Too

Strategies to help break the cycle of abuse

by

Dr. Norma Barnett

authorHOUSE

1663 LIBERTY DRIVE, SUITE 200
BLOOMINGTON, INDIANA 47403
(800) 839-8640
www.authorhouse.com

First published by AuthorHouse 05/28/04

ISBN: 1-4184-2130-8 (e-book)
ISBN: 1-4184-2129-4 (Paperback)

This book is printed on acid free paper.

Published by:

HELPING HANDS MINISTRIES
P.O. Box 66082
Heritage Postal Outlet
Edmonton, Alberta T6J 6T4

Acknowledgements

"I can do all things through Christ that strengtheneth me," Philippians 4:13.

I thank God that He has enabled me to complete this project with the help of my family. The enduring patience and encouragement from my loving husband Robert children Andrew, for his computer skills, and Chantelle for her editorial skills of this book, and for their cooperation. Special thanks to Hyacinth Barrett and Pat Saunders, for their untiring ability to decipher my notes, translating them with their typing skills. I also acknowledge Sonia Barham and Marilyn McGreer, my prayer partners for their supportive prayers and vote of confidence in my ability to accomplish this task. Special thanks to the Northwest Territory (NWT) Status of Women's Counsel for allowing me to use their statistics, and also "Changing Ways". Thanks to Greg MacLelland for his patience and computer skills.

I am equally grateful to Dr. M. Booker and Dr. G. Forward who in the nick of time discovered my talents, abilities to perform, and empowered me to complete this book. To God be the glory.

Dedication

All the praises should be given to Jesus for He has blessed me with a happy marriage. I am blessed to have grown up in the church and since the tender age of eight, I have always had a passion to help others. It is no wonder I formally pursued the nursing profession for the last 39 years of my life so that I could continue my passion in the helping profession. Being married to a minister, I have dedicated my life and time to the ministry of healing, helps, and deliverance. During this time I have observed and counseled many varied problems of abusive relationships.

For this reason I am personally and emotionally involved, and concerned about the abused. In light of this, I want to dedicate this book to churches in an attempt to raise their consciousness of the societal dilemma of violent/abusive behaviors, which is a psychological and financial burden to the social system. Abusive relationships are also prevalent in the churches whether spiritual, emotional, marital disruption or through gender issues they are silently there. The pastors, clergy and or the laity cannot continue the silence. To not speak out is to facilitate a social dilemma that must be uncovered. The first step of reducing an abnormal behavior is to openly acknowledge that there is an existing problem. The next step is to devise ways to deal with the problem.

Having said this, it would be encouraging if the pastors and leaders of churches would consider getting together for a time of discussion in an open forum to discuss the issue seriously. Possibly this topic of 'abuse' could be considered as part of the Sunday school curriculum, and or Christian Education program. Lastly, prayerfully and skillfully take the issue to the Lord. "In all thy ways acknowledge Him and He shall direct thy paths". (Proverbs 3:6).

Table of Contents

Preface

This book is presented to raise the awareness of the shocking reality of control and power that women face in our evasive society. This book will explore statistical, social, theoretical and Biblical viewpoints of sexual and physical violence in the family with the goal of providing hope and healing.

The first world was destroyed by God because of 'violence' (Genesis:6-11-13). Violence is an act of man's sinful nature which elicits the judgment of God upon mankind (Psalm 11:5-6). But there is the commandment or law of love. "Love thy neighbor as thyself" (Leviticus 19:18; Matthew 19:19). As the principle of loving our neighbor is being lived out there may be some diffusion of the quantitative violence that society experiences. Abuse is ubiquitous in the secular as well as the church world. One might challenge the degree of abuse in the church but the silence and the apathy of not exposing this is enough to qualify the idea of the monster 'violence and abuse'. Abuse and violence in the church has its own religiosity.

Researchers are searching for reasons why men abuse their partners. These reasons are found in the systems that interact with the family such as low income, unemployment, and pre-existing abusive conditions within the family of origin and the like. Psychologists are investigating why so many adolescent boys are violent at such an early age and why so many adolescent girls are suffering from low self-esteem.

Physical abuse/violent behavior is a social dilemma within the context of the family and affects every member of society in one-way or another. Family abuse is not assigned to one sector or status of society, and is not restricted to age, gender, or color. The rich, poor, educated, uneducated, every age bracket, gender and color have experienced some form of abuse as documented in research. Statistics have demonstrated to the world and the church the need for change.

Is the church aware of abusiveness within their confines? This book is written to bring about a new level of consciousness in the church and to provide a mechanism to collaborate and facilitate change within our communities. True collaboration between the church and the community can only occur if a person can rise to a new level of spiritual healing and receive therapeutic counseling at the same time. It is important that the church is cognizant of the characteristics of the abused and the abuser's behavior. I am hoping that this book will facilitate a new move giving direction to the church toward meeting the needs of abused women and provide hope and a new freedom for abused women..

There are pastors, ministers, missionaries and other clergy that can see the potential in the victim of abuse, and would like to open up the church, even though the abused woman's way of thinking has caused her to struggle through circumstances. The church does not want to use "spiritual deliverance" as a Band-Aid for emotional scars but should provide long-term counseling and guidance working through the healing process.

Within this book there are ways provided for counseling methods and modalities for treatment of abused women and specifically what the church, and clergy as a whole can do. The hope then lies in the church as being a viable institution that can offer hope and rebuilding of fractured relationships. The answer lies in unlocking the chains of fear, doubt, hopelessness, guilt, shame, scars, oppression, depression, suicide and abandonment for every young girl and woman. Where did these scars come from? How long have they been living like this? What do they remember from their youth? These are some of the questions among a host of others that the church as an institution of help and love can help to unlock with the production of a new set of "keys".

The new set of keys represent the road map to a wholesome life. The insight and guidelines of the road map is to facilitate the journey to healing and wholeness. The knowledge gained from the road map is enough to mobilize abused women to a new level of freedom through counseling and mentoring.

Throughout this book I will address some of the issues of women abuse, its impact on the abusee, the children, characteristics of the abuser, and societal views. I will investigate how society, both traditional and current, has greatly affected the issues of "Abused Women" in the 21st century and highlight the change in attitudes.

CHAPTER 1
Introduction

"Eli, Eli, Lama Sabachthani My God, My God, why hast thou, forsaken me?" (Matthew 26:47). This was a cry of despair and utter helplessness demonstrated by Jesus Christ son of the living God. Jesus, in such a position, yet found himself in such an emotional state it is difficult to comprehend, yet it is true. Is it possible that God can heal the brokenness of abused women? The answer is yes He can as there is nothing that God cannot do "With God all things are possible"(Matthew 19:26).

On the cross Jesus experienced physical, emotional, mental, psychological and sexual exploitation; that is His clothes was ripped off publicly leaving him naked synonymous with rape. His personage was violated his natural beauty marred and physically scarred (Isaiah 53:3-6). So then, to say God does not understand how abused women feel is inaccurate. He was also exploited, rejected, despised, and was acquainted with grief even as abused women are. All the people He helped, ministered to were aloof, not available or were merely observers. As a matter of fact, they did nothing to help alleviate His pain and suffering. So to say God does not care or understand the position or place of abused women is fallacy because all of the above descriptors of Jesus are equal descriptors of how women in an abusive relationship feel and experience.

The Bible says God is in touch with the feelings of our infirmities that means He is acquainted with our grief (Hebrews 4:15) and that each of our pains can be associated with His pain and suffering at Calvary. This will reiterate the last cry of Jesus "My God; My God why has thou forsaken me?" Meaning why have you abandoned me?. This is the kind of abandonment that abused women experience. Many times abused women feel abandoned by their family, friends, God and society.

This was a profound intensified emotional moment for Jesus. Physically He died and was left dead for three days but He arose. Abused women like Jesus suffers mentally, emotionally, psychologically, spiritually, and sometimes, physically. Their psyche goes through a type of deadness, numbness, dehumanization that only Jesus and themselves can truly understand.

Abused women often times feel dissociated from themselves. The 'SELF" is dead from the shock and trauma of the violence. However, with the help of counselors, supporters, prayer and divine intervention abused women can regain a sense of balance, power and empowerment – a kind of resurrection – even as Jesus did. Having obtained help from God abused women can continue and become a witness even as Paul did. (Acts 26-22). Having experienced and overcoming the horrific circumstances they can now move to another level of hope to the point where they are able to offer themselves to other abused women even as Jesus did. **'Women Helping Women' is profound as they speak the same language and have the same type of rhythm.** As the caterpillar changes through metamorphosis and becomes a graceful butterfly that surveys the world like wise there is the potential for abused women to change and fly.

This process of change involves movements – a process if you will, such as crawling, struggling, pressure, and turbulence – but all of these movements will eventually develop changes and an emergence of a new character 'a whole person' embracing a new life. How then can the 'whole person' be developed? There are some questions that must be answered concerning the notion of wholeness.

Can the Holy Spirit really heal the pain and suffering of abused women? Can the fragmented abused women be really made whole? After all, Jesus in the same predicament cried out, felt alone and forgotten by His father. How and why would Jesus be able to make abused women whole? Remember "But He was wounded for our transgressions, he was bruised for iniquities, the chastisement of our peace was upon Him and with His stripes we are healed" (Isaiah 53:5). This is the consolation 'Abused Women' that your healing and wholeness will happen because of His stripes. The answer also lies in the powerful Word of the Bible that says "It is God's will that you be in health and prosper even as your soul prosper (3 John :2).

THE ROAD MAP FOR A WHOLESOME LIFE:

Acceptance of Jesus Christ in your life
Relationship with God
Meditation and affirmation of God's word
Reliance on spiritual guidance
Knowing your limitations
Tap into your spirituality
Reaching out to others
Knowing who you are and your purpose in life.

Made in the image of God

Self worth

Self love

Self motivated

On a mission

Inner peace

Knows how to balance between success and failure

Not afraid of trying

Learn from past mistakes

Resilience

Readiness to change

Accept that change is inevitable

Ability to accept change

Sees change as an opportunity to move beyond the here and now

Ability to reflect evaluate where you came from.

Evaluate where your going

Ready to move in a forward direction

Allowing the emergence of something new.

Power of forgiveness

Forgiveness is the anecdote to healing

Sign of growth and maturity

Learning to trust self and others

Learn to trust own inner self

Learn to trust intuition

Giving permission for others to enter into your private world

Be sensitive of others needs

Be at peace with your trust

Validate your trust

Letting go of the past:

Lay the tomb stone of abusiveness and violence

Closing the chapter on the abusive relationship

Visions of unveiling the new life

In quest and search for other options

Asking the question 'what else is available'.

Renewal of your mind

Renewal of old thoughts

Flushing out of old thoughts

Releasing negative thoughts

Welcome positive thoughts

Think thoughts of accomplishment

Think thoughts of freedom

Reaching out for the newness of life

Visualize the new space

Celebrate the newness

Setting goals for the new life

Renewal of your body, soul, and spirit.

Your body as the temple of God

Visualize the healing of your broken body

Experience the freedom in your soul

Welcome happiness in your spirit

Welcome confidence in your spirit

Visualize the peeling away of the emotional scars

Flushing out of psychological pain

Knowing your gifts and talents

Internal journey to discover your gifts and talents that were

suppressed and hidden can now ooze out into the new 'you'

Share your gifts and talents with others

Celebrating your future

Having completed the journey you can now priorize maximize and celebrate your future. There is a whole future that lies ahead of a 'wholesome woman' even with her past history of abuse. There is 'HOPE AND EMPOWERMENT "for abused women.

However, family violence in our society is prevalent and is of growing concern. Traditionally the home is meant to be a safe place, a haven where families learn the internal dynamics of love, warmth, security and acceptance. Within the context of the family system each individual member learns how to express feelings, cope with internal changes, stress, and interactions of friends and families.

The family is the first institution where each member learns how to take on responsibilities, rights, interdependence of family members, rules, overt or covert; how to deal with anger and violence, role performance, societal values and the law.

It's sad to state that the traditional family unit as instituted by God has deteriorated and corroded with time, advanced technology, new innovative styles, the family of blended parenting, and the like. Also population explosion, increases in education, new political and social views on marriage have affected the family unit.

The reciprocal influences of the society, the schools and other organizations have grossly affected the family as a safe unit. As a matter of fact in many ways society has facilitated: "Women Abuse" by television programs, advertising, internet access, sensationalism of women as being sex objects, the property of men. In a nutshell there is a "Satanic Attack" against the divine injunction of the family unit. "Domestic violence is one of the most underestimated and underreported crimes in the United States today. It represents the single greatest cause of injury to women, and affects more than two million women each year. Its origins, however, lie not in the violence of our contemporary society, but in the historical subjugation of women in patriarchal societies. Traditionally, female family members existed only in terms of their relationships to men. As daughters, subject to the control and whim of fathers, women represented a means of economic or political gain through marital arrangements. As wives, they became their husbands' property, and symbols of power and status. Violence against women served to coerce their acquiescence in this scheme and perpetuate subservience to male relatives" (Bernadette Dunn Sewell, 1994).

In light of these facts, I am cognizant that the nuclear family father, mother and children as solely designed for the purpose of God has been under great siege and sabotage by Satan in an effort to destroy the unit. Many Christian pastors are too isolated from such a striking issue, a societal dilemma. My intention is to solicit pastors/church counselors and any one that is sensitive to this issue to pause, look, and investigate the issue, its effects and affects. Next explore the precipitating factors and warning signs with an effort of participation endeavoring to destroy the giant abusiveness. I am aware that women also abuse men without any prejudice or bias, but for the nature of this project, I will focus mainly on "Abused Women". Many of our Christian pastors, missionaries and lay church counselors are asking, "Am I equipped to handle these many abused situations that are frequently encountered?"

Woman has a special place in God's creation, as woman was not made from the earth but came from the ribs of the man (Genesis 2:18) "And the Lord

God said, it is not good that man should be alone: I will make him an help meet for him". "And the Lord God caused a deep sleep to fall upon Adam, and he slept; and he took one of his ribs; and closed up the flesh instead…" And the rib, which the Lord God had taken from man, made he a woman, and brought her unto the man". (Genesis 2:21- 22). When God made woman she was made whole, and placed in a pristine environment. The Woman had a place to call home with a husband as her mentor and leader.

Adam's characteristics were not those of bullying, coercing or abusiveness. The essence of Adam's leadership role was to provide support for the woman, foster a feeling of security, affection, intimacy and having relationship in worship.

Notice that when Eve arrived everything was in place. There was the garden, furnished vegetation, a place to call home, a sense of belonging. God set precedence for Adam being in the image and likeness of God to perpetuate that type of lifestyle. Furthermore, Adam was to take care of the woman being the weaker vessel. The weakness of the woman is not so much her physical structure but her emotional nurturing instinct. A woman tends to lean more to her inner emotional strains while the man appear to demonstrate more logic and information gathering. These are viewed as strikingly vivid contrast between the woman and the man, but the woman has the awesome ability to give birth and produce life. Eve, the first woman represents "Life" which means the mother of all living. This is the strength and beauty of the "woman" the man with the womb.

Adam's characteristics were parallel to God's in the affection he showed toward Eve and the care he took in looking after his own kind. He verbalized how he felt toward the gift of having a woman presented in his life from God, and not only was she presented to Adam but she came from Adam (Genesis 2:23). This made Adam feel an immediate bond with the only woman for him and from this came cleaving intimacy and trust (Genesis 2:24), which in turn made the marriage authentic. In verse 25 of Genesis 2, the final attribute we see is Adam and the woman together being proud of who they were and the state that they were presented in and this was the epitome of a bonded family. There in the garden and naked they "were not ashamed".

Adam had God, as his director. There was the beauty of the garden, and there was horizontal and interpersonal relationship with the family and God. Then Satan visited the garden home resulting in disruption of the normal flow of order. This in turn created a "dysfunctional family" with blaming and name calling (Genesis 3:12). This was the first time the concept of verbal abuse is portrayed in the Bible. Why verbal abuse? Because of the blaming and name-calling between the serpent, the woman and Adam. When God visited the Garden he was looking for the caretaker of the Garden but by this time self-degradation had set in and Adam and Eve hid themselves from the Lord.

When God questioned Adam about his disobedient actions he immediately blamed the woman, the woman blamed the serpent and the cycle of abuse perpetuated. No one wanted to face the issue of degradation and broken relationship. Adam, at this point lost the respect and bond that was first demonstrated in the early part of their marriage. Loss of identity, blaming, shame and utter chaos within the family relationship began and thus the cycle perpetuates. Satan initiated the dysfunction through the mode of deceit, lies and control. Satan positioned himself at the top of the cycle with Eve in the middle while Adam took a low position (Genesis 3:4-5) producing a most vicious cycle that still persists in families today.

The woman today is still positioned in the middle of the abuse between husband, children, family, and society. Why? If she stays popular belief is that she loves the abuse, if she leaves she fails her family. Even as the struggle continues between God and

Satan for power and control, so is the abusive man with his lover.

Verbal abuse in the garden

☞ **Satan** accuses God

Eve takes the fruit

God calls Adam to account

☞ **Adam** blames Eve

☞ **Eve** blames the serpent

The literature review states that the abusive man uses power and control to cover his own misery and failure.

As aforementioned, Satan has destroyed the family harmony and created a dysfunctional type family. Dysfunctional families experience major problems. For example one parent may drink too much or use drugs or abuse the children. In other words, a "dysfunctional" family is unable to carry out its specific duties and responsibilities. Certain members do not fulfill the requirements of their roles such as mother and father" (Valerie Lynch Lee, 1990).

Abuse is defined as being improperly used, or injurious. To hurt by treating wrongly, injured, insulting coarse language (Frank Wall Dictionary).

Abuse can be verbal, psychological, emotional, sexual, and economical. Abuse is like a snake that injects its venom into its prey and in the end devastates and kills "self and life". When a person is abused regardless of the type it's an insult, an attack at the core of the person's "SELF".

Abuse causes a person's self to be belittled, altered and less than its full worth of humanity. Abuse also produces rejection, damaged relationships, fear, low self-esteem, confusion, isolation and ultimately alienation from God. Abuse leaves emotional scars, wounds that can penetrate deep in the soul and viscera of one's personality. Damaged relationships and wounded emotions are types of captivity locked into an ocean of negativity, drowning on hopelessness and abandonment, laced with fear.

While there are many variations in the family structure God our Creator originally designed the pattern and hierarchy from the origin of time (Genesis 1:26). God's creation reflects his intentions and purpose for the family. The first parents created by God, Adam and Eve were placed in a pristine environment to grow, develop, and have harmony, interpersonal and intra-personal relationship with God.

Humans were made wholesome, complete biologically, cognitively, socio-economically, and spiritually with God being the center of the family structure. With the passage of time the serpent sereptiously crept into the serenity of Adam's home and upset the divine order and purpose as intended by God. Adam knew and understood what it meant to live in a peaceful home, experiencing harmonious relationship with God and the environment but the woman being deceived by the devil introduced disharmony and emotional abuse (Genesis 3:8). "The blaming game." No one in the family wanted to take responsibility for the act of violence an indictment against God's order. This resulted in a disassociated, dysfunctional, disharmonious, broken relationship both in the marriage and with God. This gave rise to the emergence of the dysfunctional family.

As Adam and Eve were driven out of the serenity of their home (Genesis 3:24), "the Garden of Eden" the major environmental influences greatly impacted their lives, as it does today. The school, church, and peer group influence every home. Adam and Eve now had to deal with the impact of a sinful society, raising their family through school, worship, family dynamics, and other outside influences, which would impact their lives. Urie Brofenbrenner in his approach to development uses an ecological approach. Development must be studied within a social, cultural and historical context, and is both internal and external.

Brofenbrenner's Ecological Approach to Development looks at the child's relationship with the different social environments and how it influences him. The child's environments can best be envisioned as spheres or layers and that each directly influences the other. There are a number of external forces that impinges upon each individual lives which facilitate what we become. At the center of Brofenbrenner's Ecological Approach is the Microsystem which constitutes the parents, peer group, classroom, schools, and the church. The next sphere represents the Mesosystem which consists of the teacher, the Sunday school teacher and the day care. In this sphere there is direct interaction with the Microsystems. The parents and the Sunday school teacher should network to facilitate the spiritual growth and development of the child. The teacher and the family should interact to optimize the child's educational development. The stronger and the more diverse the links among settings, the more powerful an influence the resulting systems will be upon the child's development.

The next sphere represents the Ecosystems which consists of the school board system, medical institutions, mass media, neighbors, extended family, the community and social service agencies. Within the Ecosytems the child is not directly involved but the parents are through work. However the child's development is still being influenced. The fourth and most outer sphere represents the Macrosystem which constitutes the cultural values, social conditions, economic patterns, political philosophy, and natural customs. This fourth outermost layer exerts the least influence and impacts the child indirectly. This is the layer that provide broad ideological and organizational patterns. Macrosystems are not static but can change over time based on the economic recession, technological changes and the like.

Within the context of this graphic illustration one could postulate that in any given society children that are born are subjected to all of these systems impinging and contributing to their lives in some way. For example, the first and foremost system the Microsystems or family of origin has the greatest impact on each child's life.

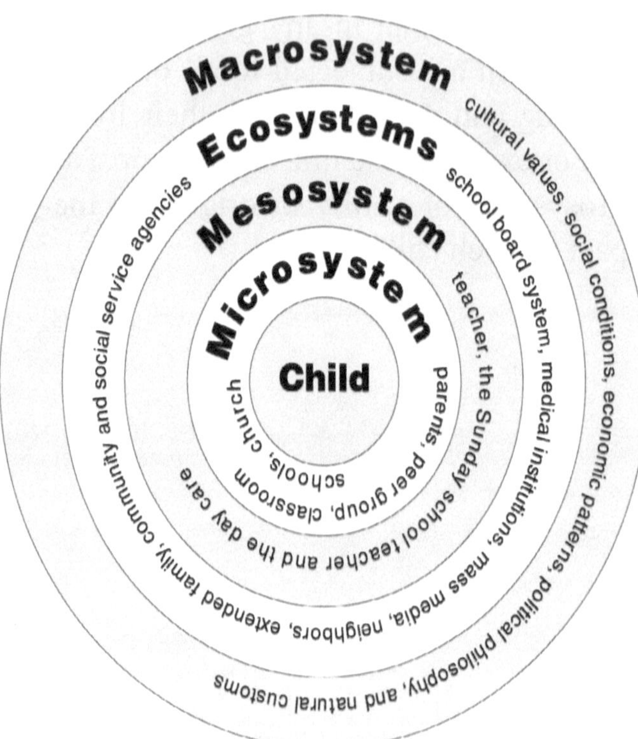

Macrosystem
Ecosystems
Mesosystem
Microsystem
Child
cultural values, social conditions, economic patterns, political philosophy, and natural customs
school board system, medical institutions, mass media, neighbors, extended family, community and social service agencies
teacher, the Sunday school teacher and the day care
parents, peer group, classroom schools, church

Depending on the family of origin whether there were two parents, love and respect, honesty in relationships, religious affiliation, caring that showed interest in the child's growth and development; or a family of violence, single parent with low economic status, low educational goals, unemployment, alcohol and drug abuse, family violence, and no support system. In light of the family and its internal practices the environment determines the potential for ongoing violence and dysfunction family habits to perpetuate. In light of this, one can visualize and understand the need for a stable family life and affiliation of the family with the church.

In the Mesosystem the affiliation of the family with the Sunday school teacher will facilitate the solidity and harmonious process of the family as intended by God. This type of environment would foster healthy man woman relationship inhibiting any type of abuse.

Where the problem arises is that many of our families are missing the affiliation with the church and the Sunday School teacher. When all the systems and all the existing parts are in equilibrium with each other the family will be the replica of the larger society. I would like to assert that without acknowledgement of God and having an affiliation with the vital Micro and Mesosystems as part of one's upbringing, it is no wonder that the family has eroded and violence, wife beatings, child abuse, emotional abuse, sexual abuse, elderly abuse, and economic abuse have plagued our society. When all of these are in place and there is the right interaction and blending of the different systems the result will generate a more healthy stable environment which eventually leads into the Macrosystems that represents the cultural values, social conditions, and political values which is the most distant layer; which most often overrides and dominates the issues of the day.

A research analyst calculated that sexual assault and abuse of women cost Canadians $4.2 billion a year in medical cost and work days lost (Priest, 1996). The Centre for Research and Violence Against Battered Women estimates that women were unable to work because of assaults and lost $7 million a year in earnings and the welfare system spends $1.8 million per year to support women who have left abusive relationships (Gurr et al. 1996: 6).

Without any bias I would like to communicate with the man who wants to be enlightened and change. However the man needs to know that he too is a by product of God's creation and that he is fearfully and wonderfully made. As a matter of fact, the man was made first then given the awesome responsibility to care for the environment and to have a relationship with nature and with God. Men you had the position of heir and stewardship to care for humanity and procreate. You knew your position as provider, gardener, farmer, and then lover and caretaker of your woman.

Having experienced loneliness for some one of like kind God gave you the woman to fill the loneliness to be intimate so much that you testified that this woman is bone of my bone and flesh of my flesh. This was ownership. Men you had intimacy with God and man, obedience to God and excellent communication with nature and with God. Your social life and spiritual life were harmonious. As a matter of fact you shared the same sexual, spiritual and physical intimacy with the woman. Having started holistically the question is raised what brought about the disruption and dysfunction? The research states that men who were abused are more likely to be abusive themselves. This will be explored later. What I would like to say and offer to these men is that there is hope for you to return to your original state, that you too can reinstate your relationship with God, that you can learn the art of healing through honesty and forgiveness. After all God is gender friendly and is willing to free the abuser from bondage. I would like to ask the man who wants to change, to take the time to read this book objectively and try to find his way back home to his original state. It can be done in light of Christian counseling and mentoring. This is the message of hope to the abuser.

HISTORICAL PERSPECTIVES

Historical perspectives relate to events that have taken place in the past and the attitudes toward women and abuse is not new. The scripture cites that "The thing that hath been, it is that which shall be, and that which I done is that which shall be done and there is no new thing under the sun" (Ecclesiastes 1:9).

Indeed abuse and violence against women is not new and even in biblical times women were classified as second-class citizens as this was rooted in the Jewish culture. In Old Testament biblical times during the age of the law and the prophets women were viewed negatively and regarded as generally less intelligent than men. Women were also seen as a source of sexual temptation. The role of women in social life was greatly diminished as well as her place in worship under Judaism. The women could attend worship but was not required to do so except on particular occasions. Women were not allowed to lead worship and were unable to do oral reading of scripture. Most rabbis despised teaching women. The Talmud collection of Jewish writings dating before Christ to the sixth century AD classified women with slaves and heathen and assumed them incapable of learning.

Plato who believed in incarnation "states that a bad man's fate would be reincarnation as a woman".

Aristotle regarded a woman as a mutilated man. Josephus a contemporary of Paul wrote that the woman is inferior to the man in every way. In Jewish law a woman was not a person but a thing.

The woman had no legal rights she was the absolute possession of her husband. It is obvious the emotional and psychological abuse that permeated the society of that era. Women were regarded less than men. Needless to say the gender bias was very blatant, the put downs, the sarcasm and the woman being an object of sex is radically devastating.

This is the epitome of psychological and emotional abuse. Even in worship abuse was present in that the woman had to be silent. Today in some of our churches this notion of the woman being silent is still prevalent; while some male pastors detest women having leadership positions.

I have visited churches where the women sit on one side of the church and the men sit on one side. I have also attended a church where the women had to sit with their husbands. The women were not allowed to say anything or read the scriptures out loud in the church. The women were not allowed to openly speak out about God and were only permitted to speak if the pastor gave permission. In other words the women had no identity. This in and of it self is prejudice and gender oppression.

The scripture that most prejudice men use to support the notion of women being silent in the church is 1 Corinthians 14: 34. This chapter essentially teaches about tongues and prophecy. Paul was concerned with the misuse of tongues and other spiritual gifts in the church. This particular problem was crucial to the church in Corinth and not applicable to all the churches although the basic principles of edification, charity and unity are fundamental to all the churches. Furthermore, there was confusion in the church with uncontrolled and disorderly manifestations of tongues and prophecy. 1 Corinthians 14-33 "for God is not the author of confusion, but of peace, as in all churches of the saints". 1 Corinthians 14-34 is very controversial today and is interpreted differently by different people.

However, within the context of the scripture at the time some writers state that Paul was specifically prohibiting women from speaking in tongues in the churches and was only restricted to men in the churches. But women are permitted to pray (1Corinthians 11:5) and prophesy in church as long as the other rules were observed (Acts 2-16-21). The women were supposed to ask their husbands questions at home and not in the church. The question comes to mind what if a woman does not have a husband who does she ask? To silence the woman in church is a notable case of divine sabotage and spiritual oppression. Women are equal in their relationship with God and do have a right to praise and worship God in the sanctuary. However, because of the nature of this book and it's intent and purpose I will now close the gate on this controversial issue of the woman being silent in the presence of her God. This is an invitation for more exploration for those who are motivated.

Despite Jewish restrictions and abusiveness toward women, Jesus Christ's attitude toward women was radically different from the Jewish custom. For example the woman of Samaria who came to the 'well' had a conversation with Jesus that was very displeasing to the Jews.

Jesus took time to acknowledge the woman and was not rooted in the law of the land neither was he gender biased.

Furthermore, the woman caught in the act of adultery was taken to Jesus by the scribes and Pharisees. According to St. John 8:3-4 the woman was caught "in the act of adultery" so it is obvious there must have been a man but there was no mention of the man being brought to Jesus. According to Leviticus 20-10 and Deuteronomy 22:22 both parties were to be put to death. The Pharisees being hypocritical and gender bias demonstrated their double standards by only accusing the woman. Jesus knowing the deceit of their hearts began to deal with the gender bias by asking the potent question. "He that is without sin among you, let him first cast a stone at her" (St John 8:7). No one was able to and they all left. As a result Jesus did not condemn the woman but offered his forgiveness and rendered her free so she could move on with her life. This is the type of freedom that is available to the abused woman.

Women were great supporters of Jesus' ministry and were allowed to preach and teach (Acts 18-26, Romans 16:1-3).

Research studies reveal that during the middle ages a woman was not able to have dialogue with her husband without the potential for her being physically abused to the point of being murdered. Also during the eighteenth and nineteenth century the heads of state, government, and church endorse the notion of wife beatings being legal as long as it was done in private.

Women were not allowed to talk back to their husbands or voice their opinions; they were treated as children and could be severely beaten. In fact if the woman would dare to talk back to her husband her name could be engraved on a brick and then used as a weapon to punish her.

These are some of the conditions that the early century women faced. However, it is therapeutic to know that the 19th to 21st century marked a paradigm shift where society and the government are now looking at this destructive behavior as a major societal epidemic affecting every fabric of the family structure.

The abuser must be aware that abuse is a punishable crime, no one has the right to abuse someone else. The abuser is responsible for his actions. The abuse cannot be blamed on drugs, family of origin, parental style, alcohol, or any extraneous variables. The message is that society and the church will no longer tolerate abuse and that women are no longer deem men's property, that women possess personal rights and legal status separate from their husband/boyfriend. Women have more access to education, own property, and right to vote, preach, teach, and have a voice. The 'woman' is not the property of the man but rather an equal to the man.

Even though there are changes in the twenty first century, wife beatings continue and is a major societal concern mainly because of the archaic rooted beliefs. Letting go of old fundamental concepts are difficult.

CHAPTER **2**

Family & Development

Understanding individual development

FAMILY BEGINNINGS:

The family is a special kind of group sometimes called the primary group, which is the basic ingredient of society. The family forms the basic unit of society and is the primary institution where we learn to live in harmony with ourselves and others, learn culture and respect for others in the group. This is the act of socialization therefore the family is the social institution which has the most profound effect and influences on its members. According to the anthropologist Margaret Mead, "the toughest institution human experienced is the family"

Within the context of the family each member experiences socialization, family dynamics, value system, communication, and how to form both intra and interpersonal relationships. Within the context of the family its members also learn the value of conscience, morality, how to deal with societal pressures and the like. The interplay within the family also prepares each individual psychologically for how each member will function either positively or negatively in society. The family structure can strongly influence the development of the individual in that it determines its failure or success in life.

Within each family group there is a certain amount of stress and conflict that is inevitable. However, there are healthy ways in which stress and conflicts can be handled. There needs to be open dialogue and healthy communication to continue the stability and permanence.

THE FAMILY THAT PRAYS TOGETHER STAYS TOGETHER

HEALTHY FAMILY CHARACTERISTICS

A healthy family is open to change and the members are free to be themselves. Each member has high positive self-esteem and feels valuable. Each family member feels free to make mistakes without undue ridicule and condemnation. The boundaries are clear and the rules are fair and flexible. This healthy family has space and time for nurturing, caring, bonding, and encourages free expression of feelings. Members are allowed to take risks, pain and anger are allowed to be expressed in a healthy environment where the other members listen with feelings and steps are taken to resolve conflict in a healthy manner.

Parental status is clearly defined and respect for each other is fostered. Positive growth and development of each member is a definite goal. The children feel a sense of security; love and acceptance, which help them, mobilize and contribute in the larger society.

SOCIALIZATION

Socialization is the lifelong process of shaping an individual's behavior patterns, values, standards, skills, attitudes, and motives to conform to those regarded as desirable in a particular society (Hetherington & Parke, 1975). The family is the most influential agent that regulates and set the stage for socialization. However there are others such as schools, work place, church, government and the like. All these agencies exert certain amount of pressure on individuals to conform to social values. Again the family is the agent that facilitates the individual on how to respond to social values, and patterns of relating to others in their world. The literature states that the primary lesson for later life relationships is learned in the infant's experience of 'attachment'. What is 'attachment'? As aforementioned, that social development originates with the establishment of a close emotional relationship between a child and a caregiver.

ATTACHMENT

Attachment' is defined as the intense, enduring, social-emotional relationship an infant forms with a parent or caregiver. 'Attachment' is not restricted to the biological parents but can also be formed with a surrogate mother. Attachment does not refer to the parents' feelings toward the child but rather a relationship sometimes called bonding. According to John Bowlby (1973), a theorist on human attachment states that infants will form attachments to individuals who consistently and appropriately respond to their signals. The attachment figure is usually the infant's mother and the signals of crying, smiling, and vocalizing are communicative signals that facilitate 'attachment'.

Developmental psychologist Mary Ainsworth did research studies on 'attachment' by putting young children in different situations such as separating them from their mothers, or introducing a stranger in the room when their mothers were nearby (Ainsworth, 1989, Ainsworth et. Al., 1978; Ainsworth & Wittig, 1969). The results reveal that the children were either securely or insecurely attached.

The securely attached children felt close to their mothers, safe, more willing to explore the environment, and challenge a new experience. There is a level of confidence in these children that if they cry out for help the missing parent would reappear.

Insecurely attached children demonstrated the behaviors of anxiety, ambivalence, and avoidance. The results states that the anxious-ambivalent children wanted human contact but cried with fear and anger during the separation. These children were very difficult to console even with the reappearance of their missing mothers. The avoidant children initially responded apathetically by showing no sign of emotion. They appeared unconcerned about being separated from their mothers, showing no sign of distress by crying, and not seeking any touch or contact on her reappearing. According to researchers, "Avoidant children may be showing the effects of repeated rejection, no longer seeking attachment because their efforts have failed in the past (Shaver & Hazan, 1994). Researchers conclude that patterns established in infancy seems to continue in many ways in childhood, adulthood, influences relationship choices, job satisfaction, intimacy experiences, and self-concepts.

Researchers have discovered that the 'attachment' behaviors developed in infancy are permeated through childhood, adulthood and even influence vocational choices, relationship choices and intimate experiences (Collins & Read, 1990; Hazan & Shaver, 1990, Shaver& Hazan, 1994). The major threat to attachment is separation and when anyone has a loss of an 'attachment' it produces separation distress, a pattern of negative emotions, mental disruption, and anxiety when an attachment figure is not available (Weiss,1975).

The same way babies cry when their parents are absent and they are in the care of a baby sitter, is the same experience that the adult survivor of abuse, divorce or intimate breakup suffers. The adult then shows sign of depression, insomnia, and needs time to adjust to the separation. It is remarkably profound that our earliest fears of abandonment and rejection can affect our lives at a later stage.

EARLY ATTACHMENT PREVENTS LATER DETACHMENT

Erik Erikson (1963) states that our social development in life passes through different stages called 'psychosocial stages or crises'. Erikson being a middle-aged immigrant to America was able to identify with conflicts that he experienced based on his new status. According to Erikson, during the continuing stage of social development there are conflicts and challenges that emerge which must be overcome, grown through, and accomplished from infancy to old age. Erikson defines 'psychosocial crises' as successive turning points or choices about self and others that influence personality growth across, the entire life span.

At each crises or stage the individual must develop a new level of social interaction through success or failure. If the individual fails or succeed it will affect the next level of development in a positive or negative way.

Erikson identifies eight psychosocial crises of which each individual must successfully overcome to be able to cope with more difficult crises in later life.

The primary crisis is vital and that is **trust versus mistrust**, which the newborn infant faces from zero birth to age eighteen months. It is crucial that the infant develop a basic sense of trust in his or her environment. This trust versus mistrust is dependent on the interaction between the caregiver and the infant. It can be the biological or surrogate mother. The issue here is the positive or negative, interaction that is taking place. The newborn infant has recently left a secure warm environment at least for nine months if there was no drugs or other toxic substance that would have passed the placental barrier. Now the infant has entered a cold open environment 'the world' where his or her future is contingent on the warmth acceptance or rejection of the caregiver. It is crucial that the infants needs are being met consistently in a positive way, thus the infant will develop a trusting relationship with the caregiver. The infant at this stage develops a warmth and closeness with the caregiver during feeding times while he or she is being breast or bottle fed.

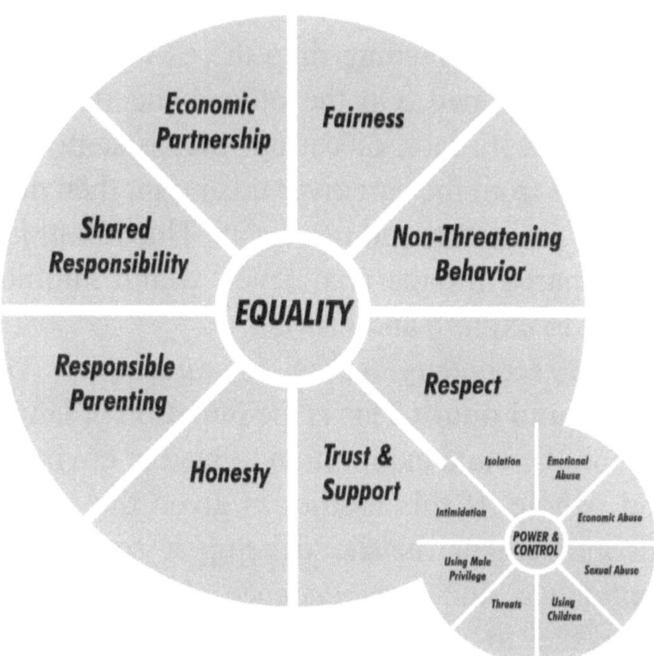

Adapted from the Duluth Domestic Abuse Intervention Project.

During this feeding time there is a bond that is being developed. On the other hand if the infant experiences a lack of caring, inconsistent warmth and love from the caregiver this infant then develop anxiety, mistrust, and insecurity. This infant is then ill prepared for the next level, which inhibits the ability to explore and grow.

The secondary crisis is **autonomy versus shame and doubt** This is the initiation of language, exploitation and exploration of his/her environment and people. If this toddler is given the space and encouragement, he/she develop a sense of self-confidence and independence. If the toddler is subjected to criticism not given the space and opportunity to explore his/her environment he/she develop the feelings of inadequacy shame and doubt.

The third psychosocial crisis is **initiative versus guilt**. This is the preschool age, which had developed the basic sense of trust is now capable of initiating tasks and being creative. If this preschooler did not develop the basic sense of trust this preschooler now demonstrate a feeling of lack of self worth. For example at this stage the child might want to do things for him or herself such as wanting to dress himself or pour his or her own juice. My grandchildren are at this stage and they often choose their own clothing and bath themselves. This initiative and independence is encouraged as it facilitates emotional growth and development.

The fourth crisis: is **competence versus inferiority.** At this stage, the child learns either to feel effective, inferior, accepted or rejected by peers. The result of failure at this stage is a sense of inadequacy, lack of self-confidence, and feelings of failure.

The fifth crisis is **indentity versus role confusion**. This is the stage of adolescence where the teenager engages in finding a comfortable sense of self that is trying to find his/her identity, testing roles, and then tries to be socially accepted. If this stage is not accomplished positively the teenager may develop a fragmented identity with role confusion.

The sixth crisis is early childhood or young adulthood and the task to be accomplished is **"intimacy versus isolation".** This is the stage where the young adulthood struggles for closeness, and intimate relationships. If this intimate relationship is not birth the individual experiences a sense of loneliness, aloneness, and denial of intimate needs.

The seventh crisis is the middle adult age **"generativity versus stagnation".** The individual is now capable of operating outside of his or her private self into the world, work, family, and grandchildren. Researchers have reported that adults who express a strong sense of being generative and productive also experiences high life satisfaction (McAdama et. al., 1993). Those individuals who have not mastered this generativity struggles with midlife crisis resolving in stagnation the battle for freedom and the desire for security.

The final stage is the late adulthood and the crisis that must be challenged is **"integrity versus despair"**. As the adult reflects on their whole life and the achievements accomplished or not accomplished, the elderly now feels a sense of accomplishment and satisfaction or a sense of failure. If there were unresolved crises and unfulfilled aspirations the individual now looks back with regrets, shame, and despair. On the other hand if the adult was successful in previous crises, the individual now feels a sense of wholeness and can leave a legacy for the next generation.

CHAPTER 3

Dysfunctional Family

All dysfunction costs. Here is a true story with factious names to conceal true identity illustrating hope and healing.

Suzy and John are a young couple who have three children, ages ranging from six to ten. They attended the same church and both are actively involved. However John was always popular as leader of one of the youth groups. For this reason John was gone on trips with the youth group away from home a lot and when he was home he did not spend much time with Suzy. He spent more time with the youth group and would often have the group over.

He expected his wife to serve these young people and never made an effort to help her with the young children. There had been incidents of physical abuse but there was more psychological abuse and neglect. Both John and Suzy had many counseling sessions from the pastor but John continued to neglect and psychologically abuse his wife.

After a while the pastor treated the situation in a matter of fact manner but there was an older elder who had experience with family counseling that intercepted. This elder took time to give pastoral godly counsel and guided the family though the scriptures how to communicate, love, share and care for each other.

With time the relationship improved and John learned how to balance his time between family and work. John also had to learn that his family needed him first before others as the family is meant to be the haven.

If your family is in turmoil then you are not qualified to help anyone on the outside. I truly believe and I know that there are many other success stories of battered women who through acceptance and reliance on divine intervention found peace and hope. There is hope both for the abusers and abused women. The batterer can be delivered from his destructive behavior.

SILENT TREATMENT POWERFUL AND INTIMIDATING

DYSFUNCTIONAL FAMILY CHARACTERISTICS

On the other hand, the troubled dysfunctional family group has the absence of many of the positive family virtues. The family structure is distorted there are no set goals or directions. Either the mother or father does not fulfill their role in parenting. Often times one parent is on illegal drugs, alcohol, or addictive to gambling. The members of the dysfunctional family are coerced to conform to certain family roles and values or there are no rules or values at all. If there are roles they are rigid and there is no room for flexibility. There is poor self-esteem and self worth. Each member must seek approval to validate their self worth. The dysfunctional family does not use problem-solving skills but rather blame each other, and openly demonstrate anger and hostility. There is a lack of trust, communication or dialogue between family members. The family structure is usually unstructured and runs in a chaotic crisis mode. Many times the children do not know where parents are. Children often times witness the abuse and if they are very young are scared, confused, and feel loss.

These children often have difficulty in school as they do not have the secure environment of love, warmth and acceptance that is so vital for the survival of its members. There are no boundaries in this household; there is the defense mechanism of denial of abuse, substance abuse, and stress. Pain becomes a way of life but there is no antidote or mechanism to deal with the pain. Reality is distorted. Many times there is financial crisis, which results in psychological and or physical abuse. Children are deprived of their basic need of food shelter and love. Adolescents are confused; their conscience and moral development are endangered related to the abusive environment and inconsistent parenting. These are the adolescence boys that will perpetuate the learned behavior of abuse and violence. These are the adolescence girls that will gravitate to abusive relationships similar to their own upbringing. This is a cycle that some authors call 'the generational curse' that can and must be broken.

I would like to further address the notion of 'the generational curse' as one of the nuances of the dysfunctional family. I am cognizant that some psychologist, psychiatrist and secular counselors may question the validity of this notion. However, it is true that some of the social maladies can be explained through spiritual insight. Psychologist and the like may refute spiritual explanations on the premise that the explanation cannot be scientifically proven. However in light of the scriptures we are all born in sin and are shaped in iniquity, but through the birth of Jesus there is hope. From the time of conception to birth and through the developmental years each person is a by product of their family genetics and traits.

HIGH EMOTIONAL COST MAINTENANCE

Each person takes on the nature of their parents, and the social and emotional environment assigned to them. As a result many of the dysfunctional behaviors such as abusiveness, alcoholism, incest, drug abusiveness, child abandonment, gambling addiction and the like are learned behaviors that have been inherited and passed down from one generation to the next. I can recall my own family of origin where there is a generation of pastors so there are positive generational behaviors that are also inherited. Some of these generational disruptive behaviors can be traced to early ancestors but the good news is that these generational disruption can be broken. How can this happen, there is the power of the Holy Sprit that has the ability to break every bondage and set every captive free.

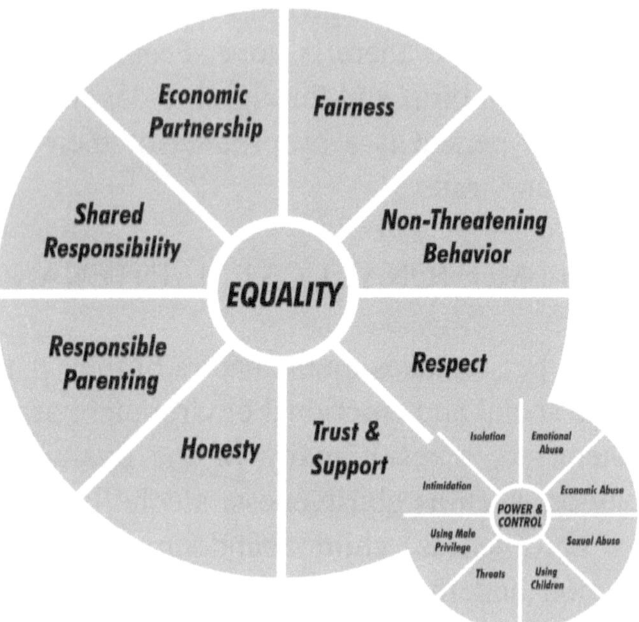

Economic
Partnership
Fairness
Shared
Responsibility
Non-Threatening
Behavior
EQUALITY
Responsible
Parenting
Respect
Honesty
Trust &
Support
Isolation
Emotional
Abuse
Intimidation
Economic Abuse
POWER &
CONTROL
Using Male
Privilege
Sexual Abuse
Threats
Using
Children

For this reason it is imperative that families in the early developmental period develop a mechanism to integrate some form of spirituality in their lives.

Within the dysfunctional family there is no latitude for communication and open dialogue. Instead there is secrecy, pain and more pain, anger that is part of the daily repertoire.

Of course there is little growth and development within the dysfunctional family and because of the denial the family head refuses to seek professional help or counseling. Many times the children who are the victims are forced to take on parental roles and are forced to grow up outside their developmental stage. Sad to state, that sometimes the innocent children are also victims of sexual and physical abuse by the abusive father. This is a family in dire trouble – 'the home of the dysfunctional family'. This is a family that needs divine guidance and protection.

Moral development

Webster defines morality as rightness or wrongness as of an action, right or moral conduct. The literature review states that one of the hallmarks of adult thinking is the development of higher levels of moral reasoning. Morality is a system of beliefs, values, and underlying judgments about the rightness or wrongness of human acts (Zimbardo P. & Weber, 1997).

Lawrence Kohlberg's (1964, 1981) theory of moral reasoning is based on a different standard of moral judgment. He defines seven stages and three levels of moral development. The lowest level of moral reasoning is to avoid pain and gain pleasure while the higher levels are based on social and ethical orientation regardless of personal gain. According to Kohlberg not every one reaches the fourth and fifth level and only a few individuals aspire beyond that. The seventh level, which is the cosmic orientation, is said to be very rare and is supposedly an ideal upper limit.

Kohlberg's stages of moral reasoning

Level and Stages   Reasons   for   Moral Behavior

1. Preconventional Morality

Stage 1:   Pressure/pain orientation   Avoid pain or avoid getting caught

Stage 2: Cost/benefit orientation;   Reciprocity ("an eye for an eye"   A c h i e v e / r e c e i v e rewards

2. Conventional Morality

Stage 3: "Good child" orientation G a i n acceptance, avoid disapproval

Stage 4: Law and order orientation Follow rules, avoid penalties

3. Post conventional (Principled) Morality

Stage 5: Social contract orientation Promote the welfare of one's
society

Stage 6: Ethical principle orientation Achieve justice, avoid self-
condemnation

Stage 7: Cosmic orientation Be true to universal principles;   feel oneself part of a cosmic
          direction that transcends-social
     norms.

CHAPTER 4
Needs

NEEDS DOMAIN

Human beings are needy individuals and when their needs are not met in a positive way, they seem to turn to other means for survival with low motivation. Maslow states that the needs at the lower level of the hierarchy dominate an individual's motivation as long as they are unsatisfied. Once these needs are attained the higher needs will become the driving focus for the individual.

According to Maslow our basic needs form a hierarchy from primitive to more advanced needs. Maslow has eight stages of hierarchial needs. The basic biological needs such as food, hunger, thirst, rest, sex and the like are fundamental to one's existence. If these basic needs are not being met then the survival of the individual to graduate to the next level is hindered. Often times the children in an abusive violent situation are being deprived of food thereby experiencing hunger. The next crucial level is for, safety, tranquility, comfort, peace of mind, freedom from fear, with the opportunity to form attachment and bonding relationships at an early age. Again these needs are most often missing from the violent families. Each individual has a need to belong, to be loved, to affiliate with others and have meaningful community support.

There is a level of esteem, where individuals begin to like themselves, to feel confident and worthwhile. The basis for confidence, a sense of worth, competence, and earning the esteem of others. There is the level of cognition, the need to know,and the quest for knowledge. Then there is the level for aesthetic needs where the individual demonstrates the order for beauty and creativity. The seventh level is the need for "Self-actualization". At the self-actualization level these persons have moved beyond the basic human needs and are aspiring to fulfill their highest level of potential. These persons are self-aware, self-accepting, are socially balanced, open to change and accepting of challenges. These persons have definite goals. There is an eighth and final step of Maslow's hierarchy of needs that reaches beyond the individual potential and taps into one's spiritual reservoir. Without the acknowledgement that there is a being that is higher, and embracing that we have a spiritual dimension, it is not possible to move into the state of transcendence or achieve spiritual connection with one's place in the universe.

Maslow's hierarchy of needs

According to Maslow, needs at the lowest level of the hierarchy dominate an individual's motivation as long as they are unsatisfied. Once these are adequately satisfied, the higher needs will become the focus.

Maslow's theory holds that our basic needs form a needs hierarchy, as illustrated. Our inborn needs are arranged in a sequence of stages, a hierarchy, from primitive to advanced goals:

The essential biological needs, such as hunger and thirst, form the base of the hierarchy. These must be satisfied before other needs can be achieved. These basic needs are not optional but are survival needs. Only when these lower order needs are met can one be motivated to meet the need for safety, tranquility and comfort. When individuals feel safe and secure they are able to move to the level of attachment. There is the need to be loved, to give love, to be

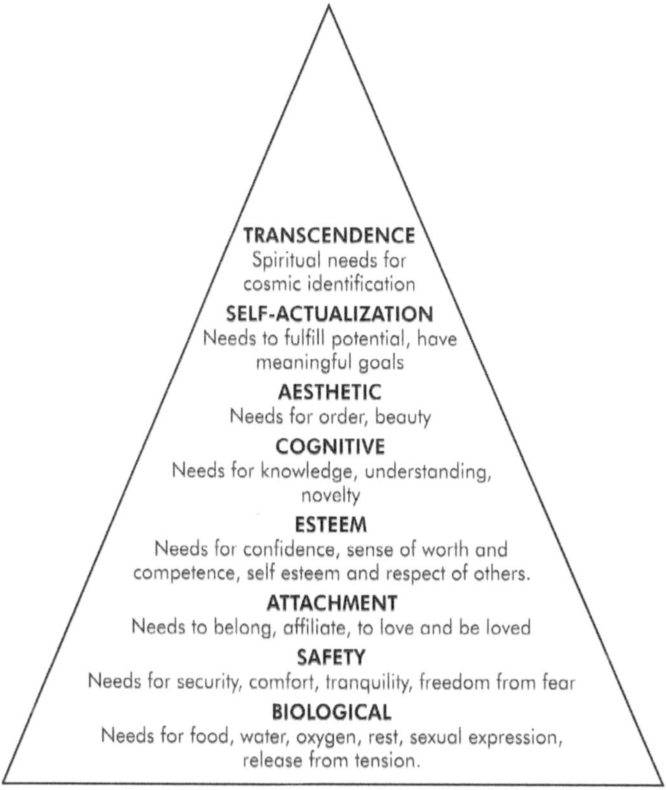

TRANSCENDENCE
Spiritual needs for
cosmic identification

SELF-ACTUALIZATION
Needs to fulfill potential, have
meaningful goals

AESTHETIC
Needs for order, beauty

COGNITIVE
Needs for knowledge, understanding,
novelty

ESTEEM
Needs for confidence, sense of worth and
competence, self esteem and respect of others.

ATTACHMENT
Needs to belong, affiliate, to love and be loved

SAFETY
Needs for security, comfort, tranquility, freedom from fear

BIOLOGICAL
Needs for food, water, oxygen, rest, sexual expression,
release from tension.

accepted and avoid loneliness. Individuals need to have interpersonal relationships as no man is an island.

Each individual has inherent worth and dignity and is valuable, therefore there is need for self esteem, liking one's self, liking others, competence, and need for recognition and respect from others.

At the next level of Maslow's hierarchy, comes the human desire for beauty and order, in the form of aesthetic needs that give rise to the creative aspect of humanity. Individuals have the capacity to demonstrate their creativity as seen in the performing arts, visual arts, music and the like.

At the top of the hierarchy are people who have accomplished the other needs and have accomplished their goals in life. These people have moved beyond basic human needs in the quest for the fullest development of their potential, or self-actualization. A self-actualizing person is self-aware, self-accepting, socially responsive, creative, spontaneous, and open to novelty and challenge. These people are now able to give back to the society and willing to share their achievement with the younger generation.

Maslow's hierarchy includes a step beyond the total fulfillment of individual potential. "The need for transcendence may lead to higher states of consciousness and a cosmic vision of one's part in the universe. Very few people develop the desire to move beyond the self to achieve union with spiritual forces." (Zimbardo Philip G, & Weber, Ann L.1997). Individuals have the intrinsic ability to transcend one's self, to connect to the supernatural and abstract to search for supernatural power. Individuals can have access to spiritual relationship as humanity is made in the image of God. "And God said let us make man in our image, after our likeness…' (Genesis 1-26).

There are varying lines of research in support of the ideas promoted in Maslow's hierarchy. A great body of work has now been assembled on people's need for relationships with others as originally postulated in Maslow's hierarchy (see Brehm, 1992; Hatfield & Rapson, 1993; Kelley et al., 1983; Weber & Harvey, 1994). The attachments people form and their reasons for seeking them can be as varied as the individuals themselves: best friendships, playmates, co-worker connections, lovers, teammates, spouses, or members of the same club. Most psychologists specializing in relationships now agree that all these different liaisons and attachments provide for our fundamental human motivation to "belong" (Baumeister & Leary, 1995). Individuals will only survive and be empowered if their needs are being met.

I have gone to great lengths to identify some of the psychological theories that might try to explain some of the reasons for the abusiveness and violence in our society. In retrospect each of the above areas can directly affect and shape each person's life to mobilize and cope with the stress and conflicts of life. In light of Erik Erikson's psychosocial stages of development, Bowlby's theory of 'attachment' Maslow's hierarchy of needs, and Kohlberg's moral development theory one can glean from each and use what is applicable to the situation they are faced with. I am cognizant that all these theories might be subjected to flaws, and are not considered a panacea for all vices. However, they are valuable tools that can be used in trying to understand human behavior.

CHAPTER 5

Abuse Defined

WHAT IS FAMILY ABUSE?

The term "family abuse" addresses acts of violence and abuse committed by one family member to another. Although researchers have used the term violence and abuse interchangeably, they address distinct types of behavior.

Violence is defined as aggressive behavior that results in injury, harm or destruction. Abuse is a broader term that refers to both physical violence and other forms of mistreatment that can result in other harm such as emotional, spiritual, and psychological.

Other definitions of abuse: as being misused, taken advantage of, or not being used for the purpose intended. Funk and Wagner defines abuse as being improperly used or injurious to hurt by treating wrongly, injured, insulting, course language to mistreat or insult.

Abuse takes many forms and the term can be defined in many ways but the overall outcome is the same. Abusive behavior is used to degrade and control the victim, deprive her of freedom to make decisions about her own life, to cause some type of psychological damage and foster dependency. That is the intent of any abusive relationship. Abuse in each case is damaging, and in many cases it leaves permanent emotional scars. Only God, who understands the hurt of the abused woman, can bring about healing and wholesomeness.

ABUSE CAN LEAVE PERMANENT EMOTIONAL SCARS

Types of abuse:

PSYCHOLOGICIAL ABUSE/EMOTIONAL ABUSE BEHAVIOR

Psychological abuse is the most devastating of all abuse in that it affects the mind, the thinking and eventually the behavior. Psychological /emotional abuse can be expressed in many ways but the goal is to control the victim's mind and thinking. In doing so, the abuser will feel like he has power, which in turn enhances his self-esteem, while destroying the self-esteem of his victim.

Psychological abuse is accomplished by verbal abuse such as name-calling, criticism, humiliation, belittling, mocking and accusing her of things he knows are not true.

The abuser sometimes tries to let the woman feel like she is crazy and it is her fault for the dysfunctional family. He yells, plays mind games, and withholds love to control or change the woman's behavior. Often times the 'silent treatment' can be very powerful and intimidating. Extreme jealousy and use of guilt is also a part of this psychological-emotional game. The woman now feels trapped and is held psychologically hostage to these negative behaviors and is paralyzed with fear. The intense fear now solidifies her insecurity and ambivalence of love as well as hate. This state is confusing as the abusive man vacillates between some kind of sick love and abuse. (Proverbs 10:11, Psalm 52:2-4).

ECONOMIC CONTROL

Economic control is the type of abuse that the man uses by sabotaging any efforts the woman makes to advance economically and educationally.

He literally withholds money from this woman so she will be at his mercy and has to beg. He will also deny her access of the car and keep her unaware of the family finances. He might blame her for the family not having enough money while he gambles or spends the money frivolously on things that he likes. Again the children are the victims and might be deprived of the basic necessities of life.

In some cases the woman works but is not allowed to spend the money she earns.

PHYSICAL VIOLENCE

Physical abuse is what most people read in the newspaper or watch on the television media but physical abuse takes many forms and often times is not reported, depending on the severity. This includes hitting, punching, slapping, pulling hair, shoving, kicking, driving recklessly, hurting the pets, scratching, choking, standing in the door way during physical arguments, using physical size to out shout the woman, assault with a weapon, keeping weapons around the house to frighten and intimidate the woman, even throwing out her personal belongings.

SEXUAL ABUSE

Sex is an intimate gift given by God to mankind for love, attachment, bonding, relationship and procreation. "Marriage is honourable in all and the bed undefiled…" (Hebrew 13-4) Sex is sacred and should be treated as such. However, abusive men use power and control to get the woman to have sex without her consent – a type of humiliation. After all, how demeaning it is for someone, after physically or emotionally abusing you, then forces you to have sex with them. This is the epitome of emotional devastation.

The abusive man may coerce the woman to have sex with his friends so he could use the incident against her in court for being unfaithful. There may be threats of guilt or other forms of manipulation. For example, Tamar was manipulated and coerced by her half brother Amnon who sexually abused her then ultimately despised and humiliated her. Amnon after satisfying his wicked sexual lust drove Tamar from his apartment with no regard for her loss of self respect or personal shame that she felt. Tamar went to her brother Absalom looking for consolation and someone to validate her feelings but Absalom also acted as if it was not a big deal, so Tamar suffered the emotional and psychological experience by her self. This is the phenomena of sexual abuse (2nd Samuel 13).

The abusive man sometimes forces the woman to have sex with him with the threatening of a weapon. There may be sodomy, unwanted touching or fondling, not respecting her privacy, performing oral sex or even sex with animals. During these times the abusive man demonstrates extreme jealousy with his bizarre sexual behaviors.

SPIRITUAL ABUSE

Man is made of body soul and spirit. The body is the outer shell that houses the spirit or the soul. The spirit man is the most intricate dimension of man. It is the spirit or inner recess of the soul that communicates with God. This is very private and must not be coerced by anyone. Spirituality is the essence of personal communication with God. This is the sacredness of your belief, which guides your path in life and gives you a sense of direction. When this is tampered with it is threatening to the core of your existence. Spiritual abuse happens when someone tries to coerce you to change your belief system to theirs, while preventing you from your form of worship. The abuser sometimes restricts the woman from participating in her spiritual repertoire. This is disturbing and can be psychologically damaging. The spiritual part of man is his or her way of communicating with the supernatural and should be allowed the freedom and latitude to maintain its development.

STALKING

Stalking is defined as one who hides or secretly pursues or follows some one. In other words the stalker is under cover. This is a violation of one's private self and is a punishable crime. The abusive man with his rage of jealousy will stalk the woman and tries to control where she goes what she does, and monitor who she is with. In one of my counseling sessions the woman shared how her husband would measure the amount of gas she has in her car and how far it would take her. This is the power of control. This abusive man often times because of his profound jealously will murder the woman. (Proverbs 1:11, 18).

Theoretical views of abusive behavior

Understanding perspectives on Family Violence assists and fosters behavioral change. Each theorist tries to unravel the rationale for violence in the family, the very fabric of society. The goal of everyone should be one of participatory guidance in helping to reduce and prevent abusive behaviours.

BIBLICAL THEORY

We live in an era of much increase in knowledge, technology, diversified family and parenting arrangements. Our society has catapulted their own vain imaginations and has strayed away from Biblical principles on how to raise a family and have wholesome harmony in the home. Yes there are many formulas, theories, and conjectures about the family but they have failed to prevent violence and abuse in the homes. Man made formulas are not lasting and although they have done much research and statistical analysis in preserving the family, it is only the families guided by godly principles that are destined to last. In the beginning of creation the Bible states "And God said, Let us make man in our image after our likeness; and let them have dominion over the fowl of the air, and over the cattle, and over all the earth, and over every creeping thing that creepeth upon the earth" (Genesis 1:25-26).

Firstly, God respects both genders Too and He gives equal amount of dominion control and leadership over the earth's inhabitants. As a matter of fact, when God addresses man the term "man" is used in a generic sense representing all of humanity.

Secondly, God made both the woman and man in His image, which denotes that both genders are invested with the same spiritual quality and have individual fellowship and relationship with God.

Thirdly, the dominion that God invested in man was not for the husband or male to be dominant or abuse the woman; but rather for the man to be under the headship and stewardship of God as he cares for his family. The man was to use all the earthly sources to its optimal, care for his wife and children keeping harmony in the home and expecting a favorable return. In (Genesis 2:21-22) God performed surgery on Adam and from him came this woman "Eve" the mother of all living. This is the first woman on the earth that brought pleasure companionship, and a helpmate to Adam. The woman came from Adam's side to denote closeness and intimacy resulting in procreation. It was God's intention for the man to first have relationship with Him, then with his wife and children, then with the larger society. To solidify closeness of wife-husband-children relationship, God further states, "Therefore shall a man leave his mother, and shall cleave unto his wife, and they shall be one" (Genesis 2:25). This is the primary inception of the nuclear family which has been dramatically changed in our society.

This is the divine principle for a wholesome family devoid of violence and abuse. The order must be obeyed even though I understand that in western culture this type of concept is refuted, and that many women characterize God and most men as being chauvinistic and patronizing. However, I am of the persuasion that this was not the intention of the Biblical theory, it is a misconception to think otherwise.

God demonstrated His love and respect for women as He likened the "Church" as His bride epitomizing the church with the character of the woman. He gave His life for the church and treats the church with such graciousness.

With the passage of time Satan tried to destroy the harmonious fellowship with God and man resulting in disharmony which disseminates to the family structure. Even though the woman is blamed for the disharmony as the Bible cites that the woman is the one that is being deceived yet in childbearing she is able to conquer. "And I will put enmity between thee and the woman, and between thy seed and her seed; it shall bruise thy head, and thou shalt bruise his heal" (Genesis 3-15).

Every woman needs to know that that she has a "Mary" inside of her (Luke 1:28). There is hope and it does not matter where she has been or what she has encountered, she is highly favored and can have a visitation from the Lord. The doors of abuse, violence and battering can be unlocked through using a new set of keys. How? by turning your battered life to Jesus he has a way of rehabilitating and healing every physical and emotional scar through the anointing of the Holy Spirit. This is the Biblical Theory of "HOPE".

SOCIAL LEARNING THEORY

The Social Learning theory states that abusive men learn to express their anger in violent ways from experience in their families of origin and are supported in doing so by societal attitudes. Many researchers have supported the notion that men who abuse their wives or dating partners have either been victimized themselves as a child and/or witnessed violence in their own family. According to the Learning theory battering/abusiveness behavior is learned. Other explanations of this theory are that the abusive man does not know how to effectively communicate and express his needs and feelings. As a result he uses violence instead of open dialogue. Secondly, he has problems controlling his own anger and again resorts to violence. Instead of expressing his anger constructively he projects it unto the more helpless, that is his partner. This allows the batterer to feel powerful and in control.

To stop family abuse should be the goal of everyone.

FEMINIST THEORY

Views sexism as the platform for men to abuse and batter their wives. According to this theory society facilitate male oppression and has given men a kind of right to control women making them powerless. Sexism is a type of discrimination against people especially against women on the basis of sex. The man's thinking is not gender friendly and he sees women as being inferior, childish and need a father to control and discipline her. With this type of warped thinking the man feels justified in using violence, control or any other destructive means to bring 'order' to this woman's life. Some cultures welcome this type of philosophy that women are inferior and are treated as such. This is a social dilemma and should not be tolerated but should be addressed with the appropriate intervention in place to facilitate changes in the man's thinking.

PSYCHOLOGICAL THEORY

The psychological theory looks at the abusers personality characters, which is different from the social learning theory. According to the psychological theory the abuser have certain intra-personal characters, which facilitates his abusive behaviors. Psychological perspectives state that abusive men's behavior is rooted in their social upbringing within the context of their family. Dutton's analysis states that the batter's violence toward his partner is traced back in part to shaming and rejecting fathers. Dutton further states, "if I had to pick a single parental action that generated abusiveness in men, I would say it's being shamed by their fathers" (1995a:83). Dutton also contributes the batterer's violence to ambivalent and angry mothers. According to Dutton the abuser's mother mixes rejection and affection in a way, which leaves him as an adult fearful of women (1995a:106). One can understand why the mother would be angry and ambivalent in her nurturing and parenting of her children. After all, the woman is also a victim of abuse and is looking for a solace for herself. Often times the woman is very fearful and emotionally distraught which causes confusion and ambivalence in her giving of herself to her children. Nurturing and emotional attachment is crucial in the early years of growth and development but the home environment has to be stable, predictable, and safe for this type of development to occur and solidify. In the absence of trust, harmony, love and acceptance it is difficult for the woman (mother) to give love constantly and acceptingly. Dutton recommends the solution is to create a therapeutic context in which abusers may understand and come to terms with these destructive patterns of responding and relating that will create new behavioral patterns. For example, in counseling the batterer would be introduced to anger management where he would learn to be in touch with his own sensitivity, in a world of feelings learning to articulate those feelings as opposed to suppressing them. Most therapists find it is more therapeutic for men to be counseled in-group.

CHAPTER 6

Effects of Abuse

A story encountered in my clinical experience

Here is a true story from my clinical experience with fictitious names to conceal true identity illustrating some of the effects of abuse.

Sarah was born in an abusive family where her mom and dad were both alcoholics. She has a brother who is two years younger. Both parents were always in combat so Sarah was a very nervous afraid shy child. Sarah was born with multiple defects in her face and had many corrective surgeries. As a result her mother would refer to her as the ugly stupid duckling and at age five her mother would refer to her as the little prostitute. She did not have many friends and had to take care of her mom as well as her younger brother. Sarah's dad was hardly around as he was a truck driver, but whenever he came home there was combat at home.

Sarah said her mother was diagnosed as having a bipolar disorder so she was on anti-depressant and was always in bed for the most part. At age six her mother had a nervous break down so Sarah ran the whole gamete at home. During this time Sarah encountered different father figures. These were her mother's boy friends who basically and repeatedly sexually abused her. Sarah's mother never once intervened or came to her rescue. Instead she had a lot of physical beatings from her mother.

At an early age Sarah experienced all the underpinnings of a dysfunctional home environment. She was physically, verbally and sexually abused. At the age of 13 her mother, in one of her drunken stupors, violently beat Sarah. This time Sarah ran away from home and took to the streets in one of the metropolitan cities in Canada.

Developmentally she had no skills to work or look after her basic needs as she was utterly deprived of this luxury. The street became her home, so very quickly as a means of survival she became friendly with prostitutes who mothered and nurtured her. She was introduced to prostitution, drugs and alcohol. After all, Sarah was never nurtured, loved or cared for so prostitution and drugs were a form of love.

During this time she had more physical abuse from gangs and the like.

With divine intervention she was adopted by a family who nurtured her, gave her security and got her back on track. During this time Sarah had no contact with her mother or her sibling. Sarah was always in search for her father so she preferred older men and eventually ran off with a man 31 years older when she was 17.

Sarah moved in with this man who treated her like a queen. He was a very successful business man who traveled a lot and would dote on Sarah with material gifts. Her apartment was well furnished and she had money. For Sarah this was the first time she ever felt 'real love'. At the age of 18 this man proposed marriage to Sarah and presented her with the most beautiful engagement ring. Sarah graciously accepted the offer and the ring. Up until this time there were no beatings.

Sarah returned to school and every thing seemed fine. Life was kind of worth living. Then came the shift in Sarah's life. Sarah had to announce to her fiancé that she was expecting their first baby. Her fiancé was outraged and he then resorted to the verbal abuse, name calling, put downs, and eventually battering. Sarah was kicked, slapped and punched around mostly in her head and face. She was told to abort the baby or he would get rid of her.

Sarah was distraught and battled with the idea of running away as she wanted to keep the baby. Sarah felt like this is the only thing that would be really hers. With much beatings and contemplations, Sarah decided to abort the baby and she eventually had three abortions which ultimately affected her psyche. Sarah had a major depressive episode, tried suicide on several occasions from alcohol and drug over dose but always the hand of God was there and she would be rescued over and over.

Sarah managed to stay in the abusive relationship for three years and had to seek psychiatric intervention. After being stabilized on antidepressant and other drugs Sarah met a Christian friend who invited her to a Bible study group at the church. Sarah went for a few times but when her fiancé found out where she was going he would violently beat upon her and accused her of just wanting to meet other men.

The physical, psychological and verbal abuse escalated and one day when Sarah came home her fiancé severely beat her in the head and left her bleeding. No one came to her rescue even with her screaming and pleading with the batterer. Sarah, now unconscious, was left in a pool of blood to die as she asphyxiated on her own vomit.

Again divine intervention was in play. Someone passed by her apartment, saw her door opened, walked in and found her lying unconsciously in the kitchen. This good Samaritan person called the ambulance and she was taken to the hospital with multiple bruises from the battering. Sarah was hospitalized for one month. During this time her fiancé never visited her once or enquired about her welfare.

Sarah was advised to press charges but she was afraid and did nothing. The ladies group from the church was the only support system that Sarah had, and so after she was released she was able to move in with one of the church family who took Sarah under their wings, introduced the love of God to her and basically mothered her back to emotional and physical health.

During this period Sarah had many counseling sessions and had to learn how to work through her early childhood years, deal with conflict, the hatred for her parents, especially her mother, and all the insults of life.

Sarah battled through counseling for at least two years and at times she was mad at God for allowing her to experience such hell at an early age. Sarah had very low self-esteem, or may be I should say none. She even struggled with the notion that God would love her. Sarah would say things like, "how could God love someone who is so unworthy and done so many bad things."

Through counseling, patience and the introduction of her spirituality, the notion of her being made in the image of God began to take root. It took continued reiteration that God loves everyone, no matter what they have done or where they have been. "For God so loved the world, that He gave his only begotten son, that whosoever believeth in him should not perish, but have everlasting life" (John 3:16).

Sarah needed constant reassurance that the battering was not her fault and that no one deserves that kind of treatment. Sarah was introduced to the notion of how the new relationship with God could help her work through some of the struggles she encountered. Sarah was also counseled through the philosophy that everyone is worthy, belongs, and has worth. "For God sent not his Son into the world to condemn the world; but that the world through him might be saved." (St John 3:17). It was very important for Sarah to know and then conceive that even though her biological father abandoned her that there is a heavenly father who loves, cares and has not condemned her.

This was also a difficult concept for Sarah to grasp. Through psychotherapy and much supportive counseling, Sarah was gradually reintroduced to society. Another difficult area in counseling was helping Sarah with self worth, self esteem and self acceptance. Sarah hated her self, had a lot of guilt and constantly would blame herself for the travesty of her life.

She had to be reminded of the power of the Word. "I will praise thee; for I am fearfully and wonderfully made…" (Psalm 139:14). Through unconditional positive regard, empathy and the reinforcement that God loves and can change situations Sarah's life began to shape in many positive ways. There were many curves, and ups and downs through out the whole process. She gained strength and confidence as she voluntarily enrolled in a number of work shops, namely: Self Esteem, Knowing Your Worth In God, Who Am I, The Secret Self, Healthy Relationships and Over coming Hurts.

Sarah had many counseling sessions coupled with mental health intervention which she relinquished over time. With the transition of time Sarah returned to school and successfully pursued her educational goals. Sarah still has no contact with her father or brother, and limited contact with her mother. Sarah is now happily married to someone who truly cares for her.

For the first time Sarah says she has truly met some one who love and accepts her as she is with all her past. Although she still has medication for her nerves, she is able to cope with the trials and insults of life without running or

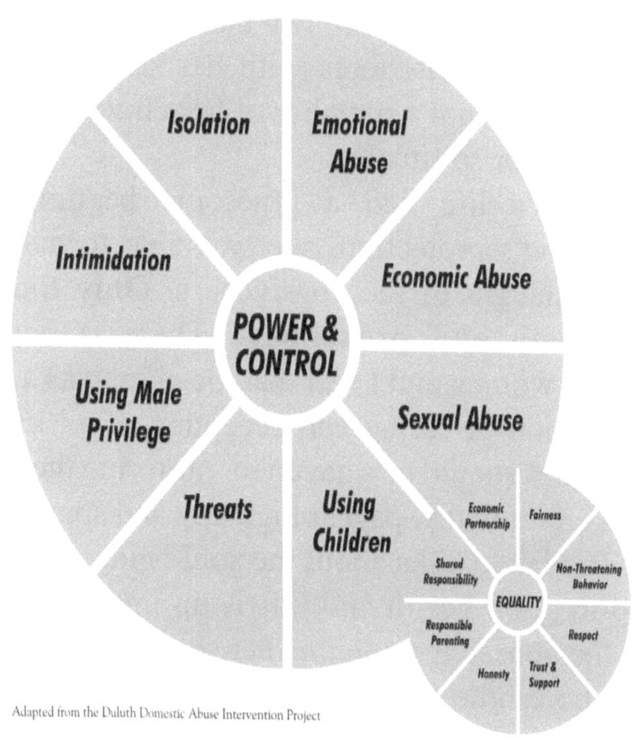

Adapted from the Duluth Domestic Abuse Intervention Project

resorting to drugs, alcohol or prostitution. Sarah has found a solace in her church group and her spouse never interferes with her spirituality even though he is not a member of her church group, he respects her spirituality.

Sarah's life had a gruesome beginning but with God's protection, she was able to overcome the onslaught of the abusiveness. **Only time can heal pain and brokenness.** There is hope for abused women and I feel that the church as a viable instituition of caring and accepting of all kinds of casualties should be a haven for nurturing the abused both emotionally, psychologically and spiritually.

The Bible talks about the soul being prosperous and in good health and this is an important factor for the abused woman that her soul, mind and spirit be wholesome that the chords that are broken can once more vibrate. That she will be able to sing a song of hope, experience freedom both spiritually and psychologically. It can be done and there is "HOPE", "NO MORE ABUSE"

HOW VIOLENCE AFFECTS THE WOMAN

Violence affects the wholeness of the abused woman. The self esteem, the thinking, the feeling and the ability to love is affected. These are some of the more common characteristics found in the abused woman.

· Low self-esteem. This woman thinks very little of her self and views her self as not being able to achieve or be anything worthwhile in life. This woman sees herself as a failure and sees her future as being a failure.

· Accepts criticism and ridicule from her partner as if it is true.

· Blames her self for her partner's destructive behaviors and thinks that if she change may be he would change. The woman needs to be educated that she has no control over the abusive man's behavior

· Society sometimes helps to solidify the belief that the woman must have contributed to the abuser's violent behavior. Also societal stereotype is that the woman is responsible for the family's welfare. This is often times the gender bias that is perpetuated in our society as the abused woman incorporate that thinking in her belief system she begins to loose power and control.

· Ambivalent in seeking help

· Distorted view of man-woman relationship

· May have rigid view of gender roles

· Often times very dependent on the batterer even though she is a victim.

· Sees no way out.

· Allows the abuser to control her thinking as she thinks he knows what is best for her and the children.

· Social isolate sometimes even from her own family of origin.

· Emotionally dependent on partner

· Denial of the abusiveness in her family. Denial is the first line of defense mechanism used to protect the self from pain. When faced with a traumatic or disconcerting experience it always seems safe to deny the reality. The abused woman may also have memories of her past stormy upbringing that would be a plausible reason for denial. Other reasons for the denial may be shame and guilt.

· Develop health problems, which are often times psychosomatic in nature.

· Depression, anxiety and fear are usually present

· Mental disorientation and suspiciousness

· Indecisiveness and inability to make decisions

· Some women resort to substance abuse themselves as a means of coping.

·   Experience insomnia and sometimes nightmares resulting in heavy use of tranquilizers.

How violence affects children

According to researchers children who grow up in violent homes have increased risk of behavioral and developmental problems. There is a greater risk of them becoming victims and perpetrators of violence themselves. These children are more likely to be sexually abused, sometimes by their own abusive parent.

Other behaviors demonstrated by abused children are aggressiveness, passivity, withdrawing and clinging. Often there are problems in the school with truancy, low grades, fighting, and being a social isolate. Sometimes these children have problems with the law, and may become partakers of adolescence date battering. Again these young adolescent boys learn violence at home and often were victimized themselves and perpetuate the learned behavior.

These children often have to be parenting the parents and take responsibility for caring for younger siblings. This is called role reversal and has forced these children to grow up too quickly being deprived of their childhood development.

They may experience nightmares, insomnia and bed-wetting. These children are often fearful, as most of the beatings seem to occur in the nights. The children have difficulty trusting others. Secrecy is usually a part of their family structure because of the shame and stigma attached to the abusiveness.

They may exhibit co-dependent personalities, experience physical complaints such as headaches, stomach problems, chronic colds and allergies.

These children are very high risk for substance abuse and some suicidal ideation because of depression. It is important that individuals learn the warning signs of an abusive relationship, that they might be able to quickly help someone in that toxic relationship.

As I attended many workshops on abused women I have developed a sensitivity and caring for these women who are subjected to this dilemma. Having sat in the workshops, attended retreats and worked with abused women I realize the importance of early detection of the clues that a woman and her children might be in an abusive relationship. It is educational to attend these workshops and participate in the action to stop family violence and abuse. Appropriate intervention can be initiated and reduce the damage.

These are some indicators or clues that will alert pastors or anyone who would like to help someone in an abusive relationship. There might be a track record of violence, which is the most accurate predictor. If the husband has a history of assaulting his partner, it is almost certain that the abuse will occur again, especially if he never had treatment. Researchers say that most abusive men do not seek counseling and will only attend if coerced to do so, or they are afraid of the law or loosing their spouse and children.

· May experience fear and phobias

· Demonstrate compulsive behaviors

· Seems to have no real purpose in life having no goals or direction.

· Abused as children or who grew up in a violent home are more likely to be victims or perpetrators.

· Loss of spiritual identity as the abuser may coerce them in changing their spiritual belief or prohibit them to attend any religious venues. The woman might loose her confidence in God in that He did not protect her and has allowed the perpetrator to abuse her. This helps to facilitate her loss of spiritual identity.

· The adult woman might not have any recollections of childhood abuse. This painful experience might be buried so far in her unconscious that it is hard to retrieve.

Self blame and denial is a definite indicator of an abusive relationship.

· Always making excuses and covering up for the abuser. For example, the woman might have an obvious scar on her face or neck but she will try to give a plausible excuse to keep from exposing her partner. **This is the dilemma of the abused woman as she demonstrates that martyr like personality.** The abused woman does not have the power to speak; out against the injustice that is being done to her by the perpetrator because she is afraid of more beatings and afraid of loosing him and her children.

· Her partner may pressure her to do things that make her uncomfortable

· Partner may use anger and threats to get things done his own way

· Shows no feelings for her emotions and rarely listens to what she has to say. Her partner may also refuse to accept her limits around sexual activity.

If at all the woman discloses any of these irregularities to a friend, pastor or anyone they should not act aloof or pretend it is not happening. Many times the abused woman will go to her Christian leader first who may negate and trivialize her story. To ignore this woman's story and cry for help is to deprive humanity of respect and sanctity. **Deprivation could cost her life.** It is imperative that church leaders be aware, alert and be honest of a real social dilemma that is also inside the confides of the church.

Common characteristics of the abuser

Researchers have found that over half of those men who are violent to their partners also abuse their children. Common characteristics of abusers are:

- Low self-esteem
- Low self-worth
- Poor communication skills
- Poor impulse control
- Strong needs to control
- Tendency to blame partner, alcohol, or other drugs
- Sexist ideation, thinks the woman is inferior and deserves the beating to set her straight
- Uses sex as a way of power and control to cover and hide his own insecurity
- Demonstrate angry outbursts
- Very jealous
- Possessiveness
- Egocentric

- Emotional immaturity
- Rigid views of woman-man relationship
- Denial of his responsibility
- Product of abusive family
- Unstable relationship with his mother
- Experience conflict with his father
- Difficulty defining love

Risk factors

ALCOHOL

The Canadian Violence Against Women reported in one of their studies that perpetrators had been drinking in more than 40 per cent of violent incidents against women, and that drinking was most likely in cases of violence involving intimates (boyfriends, dates, and spouses) (Statistics Canada 1993:5). (Duffy, Ann; Monitrov, Julianne).

Most research analysts agree that alcohol plays a part in abusive violence but does not cause violence and that the violence will not stop when the drinking stops. Alcohol and drug use more or less provide men with a "socially accepted time out" reducing inhibitions and escalating the severity of the violence. Many men who are abstainers or moderate drinkers assault their wives and many "heavy drinkers" were not under the influence when they beat their wives (Johnson 1996:55-58). Many other literature reviews on women abuse, assign alcohol as playing a major role that contributes to the violence. Abused women have testified to the fact, that many times the abuse occurs when the man is under the influence of alcohol. The alcohol helps to give more control and power as his inhibitions are removed.

The abuser uses alcohol as a crutch for his violent action, but the alcohol does not cause the violence. Other illegal drugs are sometimes used by the abuser, they do not cause the violence. Most times the abuser uses alcohol as a means of coping with conflict and stress.

PREGNANCY

Other researchers have documented that over the last 30 years one in five women (21 percent) that had been interviewed by the Canadian Violence Against Women Survey (CVAWS) reported that they experienced violence by a previous or current partner during their pregnancies (Statistics Canada 1993:4, also MacLeod 1980). These findings are interpreted based on the women's increased dependency, vulnerability, fear of the batterer increased family responsibility, and the like. Other risks factors are chronic unemployment, and witnessing violence as a child. Witnessing violence as a child has a high probability of repeating the abusive behavior.

CHAPTER 7
The Cycle of Abuse

Generally abuse follows a cycle of tension, explosion, honeymoon that keeps repeating. Here is a true story with factious names to conceal true identity that illustrates the cycle and that it can be broken.

Portia is an educated school teacher who left home at an early age but managed to earn a college education. With the passage of time Portia met Josh at the college graduation where they fell in love at first sight resulting in marriage. The honey moon was fantastic and Josh and Portia had a good relationship for the first year.

With the passage of time Josh started to come home late and was always finding fault with Portia's cooking her dressing and she could not do any thing right for Josh. At first Portia thought it was just that Josh is too tired from work plus traveling but with time things got worst.

The relationship got worst and so did the psychological abuse of name calling and put downs. Portia on several occasions said to Josh that they both should seek counseling or at least talk to her pastor. Of course Josh said he did not have a problem that the problem was Portia.

Portia lived every day in fear of the unknown and attended work and church in silence and shame. Portia then started to attend the women's prayer group and developed enough courage to disclose the verbal abuse to one of the ladies in the prayer group. The content of the prayer was that Josh would give his life to the Lord, for the abuse to stop and the relationship to improve.

Instead of Josh improving he decided to move out and live on his own. Portia continued to attend the church as that was her only support system. There were no children involved from the union. After about two years of not hearing from Josh, Portia received a phone call from Josh saying that he has changed and wanted to meet with Portia. Portia was very apprehensive not knowing what to expect after the gap in time but decided to meet Josh at a local restaurant.

Josh said he was sick and had a near death experience and how he believed God gave him a chance to live. This experience gave Josh a different outlook on life and he repented of the times that he abused Portia. Portia decided to give Josh another chance to be a part of her life and she allowed him to move in with her. Surprisingly enough Josh asked about Portia's church affiliation and he started to visit the services with Portia. After a few services Josh decided to give his heart to the Lord, got enrolled in the discipleship class and enrolled in the anger management class for men that batter their wives.

Both Josh and Portia went for family counseling with good results. Josh and Portia worked on the anger management exercises. As a result they both were able to communicate and work out their marital conflicts in light of God's word instead of using abuse. It is true that the Holy spirit and godly guidance can teach even abusive men how to treat their wives and children. There is hope and not all abusive relationships have to remain in the cycle.

Cycle of abuse by the abuser

According to research, violence does not happen in a vacuum but rather in a cycle. It is important for anyone who desires to help stop the abusive syndrome to understand the nature of the cycle. Also the more often the abuse, the greater the chance of the abuse reoccurring.

Phase 1 of the cycle is **tension building.** The tension may be the result of a petty disagreement, constant arguing or even giving each other the silent treatment. The woman is usually aware when tension is building in the relationship. The woman having been battered before knows the warning signs and tries her best to not push her partner or do anything that would escalate the tension. This stems from her fear of an explosion.

Phase 2 is the **volcanic stage**. The tension continues to escalate like a volcano with an explosive eruption at which time the physical beating, kicking, punching, slapping or even the use of deadly weapon occurs. This is the time when sexual abuse become part of the abusive play. At this time the woman experiences a number of emotions. She experiences great fear, agitation, numbness, shock, anger, and a sense of hopelessness. The woman often blames herself and thinks if she did not behave a certain way this would never have happened. Some women leave at this time, while some women try to defend themselves by using deadly weapons.

Phase 3 is the **Honeymoon Stage**. Following the volcanic battering phase is the 'honeymoon' stage, which is paradoxical to the volcanic phase.

'ABSURD'. This is the phase that the abuser tries to be romantic, loving, apologetic and contrite. In other words the abuser tries to ask for forgiveness, tries to say he is sorry and that it would never happen again. Of course the woman has heard that many times with the same type of negative result. During this phase the woman is vulnerable to believe the lie and even make concessions for him, deceiving her that he is not such a bad man and because the woman wants to be loved she willingly accepts the warp affection. This time the batterer uses sex as a way of making contrition for his violent acts. The woman often is afraid of being alone and welcome the intimacy in the relationship.

However, with time the violence reoccurs and a new cycle of violence begins.

The literature states that over time the abusive cycle increase in frequency, honeymoon phase becomes shorter and may not even be part of the abusive cycle. Some women turn to alcohol and drugs. The woman needs to be educated that true love never hurt. What the batterer took as love is more guilt. "Husbands love your wives even as Christ also loved the church, and gave himself for it" (Ephesians 5-23).

How can a man beat his wife and then expect to make love to her, **such absurdity**.

Why women stay in abusive relationship?

Women stay in the abusive relationship for different reasons depending on her culture and childhood experiences. According to researchers cultural issues

The cycle of abuse

Adapted from L.E. Walker

may be a factor in that the woman might have grown up in a patriarchal society where the man is the head of the household he has the power to rule and make all the decisions. The woman merely carries out and does what she is told and is expected to do so without questioning. The adult woman is reduced to the level of a child. The woman's mother did not leave during the abusive situation therefore the abused woman sees no need for her to leave. Her mother did not leave therefore she has made her self feel comfortable to stay. After all society expects her to stay. There may be socio-economical reason why the woman stays. The woman might not be financially stable or she might not be educationally prepared leaving her fewer options. She must stay and be dependent on the abuser.

During my experience with abused women I have met women who are educationally sound but have developed an emotional dependence on the abuser that even though they are educated and earn enough to support themselves they stay in the abusive relationship. It is beyond the thinking of an outsider to rationalize why women stay in such caustic relationships. To understand, one would almost have to go inside the abused woman's head and try to decipher her decision to stay. It is beyond an outsider.

·   Society also expects the woman to stay as if she leaves she has failed and if she stays it is said she must love being in the situation.

·   There might be religious and spiritual beliefs. Some religions have no provision for divorce or separation and women are believed to be family caretakers so they are expected to stay.

·   Women might stay because of health problems.

·   Immigrant women are even more susceptible to male violence and having a disadvantage of not knowing the language and being afraid of deportation have no choice except to stay and suffer.

·   Disabled abused women are also very vulnerable and also have very little chance of leaving. The disability puts the woman in a disadvantaged position. Who will advocate for her? Where will she go?

·   Fear of punishment by the perpetrator

·   Fear of losing her children

·   Fear of harm to her friends and family members

There is one incident that I recall of an abused Christian woman whose spouse left her and the children and had engaged in many affairs. With time he developed AIDS with his pernicious life style.

Of course he found his way back home. At first the emotionally distraught woman refused to take her husband back but was counseled by her clergy that she should take him back. With total obedience this abused woman allowed her husband once more in her life. As the abusive man demanded sexual activity he knowingly and surreptitiously transmitted the deadly disease AIDS to this helpless woman. The power and control of the abuser was once again reinforced, which participated in the demise of the powerless abusee "the woman". It is this type of power and control that the abused woman is faced with which must be stopped before it kills.

For this reason it is imperative that leaders listen to abused women and their children as they try to cry out for help; they have a story to tell. Allow them to tell their story in an atmosphere of safety 'the church'. You must not negate or trivialize their story it is a cry for help and the church should be a safe place for these victims.

Abused women are trapped and need to know that there is hope in God that he has the answer for their problems.

Why does she leave?

According to different researchers the woman usually leave for fear of danger for herself and the children
·   Woman hopes to support herself on her own.
·   Woman has developed some self confidence and wants to try and make it on her own
·   Woman wants to test the outside environment
Why does she return?
·   The Woman has developed an emotional attachment on the abuser.
·   Woman believes his promises and fears his threats
·   Feeling guilty of breaking up the family
·   Feelings of worthlessness
·   Fear of loneliness
·   Not having any skill or formal education
·   Lost her support system because of the abusers' control in choosing whom this woman is allowed to socialize with.
·   Financially unstable

- Believes the negativism about herself
- Feelings of hopelessness
- Upon return the woman will test the relationship and tries to have a fresh start.
- Woman hoping for resolution
- Flash back of violence may disturb and plague her
- Low self-esteem

CHAPTER **8**

Prevention/Intervention

What individuals can offer

According to researchers the abusive/violence is a cycle that gets worst each time and to change the violence is a long term process. Society as well as individuals are becoming less tolerant of this offensive behavior and may seek to assist in diffusing the behavior. There are some steps that individuals, church, and communities can contribute to prevent abusiveness in families.

For individual involvement:

·   Instill positive sense of direction and self worth in the young person by becoming friendly.

· Try to understand their developmental stage and the tasks that are to accomplish

· Try to understand their language and their way of thinking

· Try to understand the peer pressure that they face

· Show respect and help them to feel accepted

Accepting young people regardless of their behavior, a type of "Unconditional Positive Regard" as stated by Carl Rogers. You do not accept the negative behavior but you accept the person and then try to understand the reason for the behavior. In trying to understand the reason for the behavior you will open an arena for communication and dialogue whereby the adult might gain some understanding of the negative behavior, ultimately providing new behavioral patterns for this young person to adopt. As a matter of fact that is why Jesus is able to love all of creation regardless of how sinful we are. Jesus loves all of us unconditionally that is why he died for all of us. It was "Unconditional Love".

· Design a vehicle to facilitate and foster positive behaviors through role modeling. This is the dilemma. Our young people do not have many positive role models to chose from, as there is an escalation of moral decadence. Purity, morality, chastity, honesty, and trust are all on the decline. Many of our young people are confused, as there is inconsistency in positive role models.

·	Provide opportunities for young people to learn how to express themselves and deal with conflict, and anger in a non-violent way. After all, many young people are from violent homes where their parents were abusive and aggressive. Social learning theory states that behaviors are learned and these behaviors become a part of their repertoire of behavior. When faced with conflict they resort to violence instead of problem solving and good communication. That is what they have learned in their family of origin. These behaviors can be unlearned if given the right guidance and therapeutic atmosphere.

·	Respect their ability to make decisions that are positive and meaningful.

·	Provide a therapeutic environment where the young person can develop trust and foster a positive relationship with adults and others.

·	Educate young people on date violence

·	Provide spiritual guidance

·	Teach them that love is caring and sharing. Love does not behave un-seemingly

- Teach them that love is a process and that it should be allowed to evolve and cannot be coerced.
- Love does not control, punish or stifle.
- Love makes room for the other to grow.
- Teach them forgiveness to promote healing
- Teach them that they should practice the principle of esteeming others higher than themselves and that God loves freely. "Let nothing be done through strife or vain glory: but in lowliness of mind let each other esteem other better than themselves Philippians 2:3)
- Educate them that jealousy, power and control is a spirit that shows a sign of weakness and insecurity.
- Educate them that the law does not tolerate violent aggressive behaviors and is a crime punishable
- Teach them to take responsibility for their actions
- Take responsibility to report any suspicion of abuse in families

Prevention contribution in the community

Webster's dictionary defines community as any group living in the same area or having same common interests. Most communities in North America have a kind of community solidarity, neighborhood watch to prevent crime and maintain serenity in that locale. As a community member the greatest gift one can offer is the 'self' even as Jesus did. How can you offer ones self in the community? Through volunteering your time to work with troubled youths, hostels, women's shelter, prevention of crimes at the local police station, fostering a youth.

Offer to work with immigrant families who are new to North America and are disadvantaged of the language, faced with unemployment, and adjustment to a new way of life. All these stressors can precipitate an abusive episode.

- Linkage with community hospital programs
- Programs that offer education to abusive men in areas such as Anger Management. For example how to identify the triggers that precipitate the rage, how to

diffuse a heated argument, how to take time out and so on.

·   Problem solving on how to identify problems and develop positive ways of dealing with the problem that is non-violent.

·   Other programs such as financing and budgeting, parenting, marriage and the family.

·   Substance abuse

·   Communication skills

·   Provide programs for abused women and supportive therapy

·   Teach self-acceptance,

·   Programs on self-esteem

·   Preparation on vocational issues

·   Possible to continue her education

·   Educate abused women of their legal rights

·   Educate abused women of the abusive cycle and knowing when to leave in the first phase before the explosive phase

·   Educate abused women never to go in bathrooms or behind doors when there is tension as they can be trapped in the event the situation become volatile

·   Provide support for the children

· Educate abused women of the community resources and Address of emergency shelters

· Educate how to allocate the resources
· Educate on government funding
· Offer spiritual guidance
· Support programs
· Government support agencies
· Legal resources
· Multicultural centers
· Food banks

The churches role

· The church is a viable institution that communicates God's love
· Unlocks hurting past and introduce freedom through the love of God
· Assists in rebuilding damaged life
· Offering workshops on Anger Management, Problem solving strategies, Coping with life difficult situations, How to accept Christ as their personal Savior, How to have a relationship with God
· Church to be aware of the reality of abusiveness in relationships
· Awareness of abusiveness even in Christian families

·	Gain knowledge and research the problem of abuse and violence

·	Liaison with community services to offer workshops on Family Dynamics.

·	Offer premarital counseling

·	Educate the congregation about abusiveness and violence

·	Encourage openness to speak out on Family violence in small groups

·	Invite personnel from government and or social services to give information on the subject of violence and abuse

·	Preventative family violence through Biblical teachings and study of God's word on the family. For example, how God liken the church as His bride and how He cares for the church.

·	Teach equality between genders

·	Offer therapeutic supportive counseling

·	Provide safety for abused women and their family

·	Promote family education courses

·	**Educate, Educate, Educate.**

Implications for the church

·	The church should be visible in the community
·	The church can volunteer at shelters
·	Participate in training, set up abuse hot lines, and offer donations to the food bank
·	The ultimate goal of the church is to offer, hope and salvation to both the abused and the abuser. The church also aims at reintroducing the 'whole person' through godly teaching. In other words, teaching each person of who they are in light of the scriptures that each individual is fearfully and wonderfully made (Psalm 139-14), and that each person has a place in the kingdom of God. That each person is worthy.

ABUSE AND VIOLENCE IS PREVALENT IN OUR SOCIETY AND IS NO RESPECTER OF FAMILIES OR ETHNICITY.

PROGRAM INTERVENTION

Regardless of the type of program implemented the basic principles are the same.

1. Set goals that are obtainable with the client
2. Goals must be evaluative
3. Goals must be qualitative
4. Atmosphere must be motivational
5. Attitudinal change must be encouraged
6. Christ centered approach
7. Client centered approach
8. Knowing when to make the appropriate referral

CRISIS INTERVENTIONS

Crisis means both danger and opportunity. Crisis is dangerous when it threatens the normal emotional equilibrium to the point that a person's adaptive capacity is no longer adequate to deal with the crisis (Aguilera, C. Donna). During times of crisis a person is more open to accept assistance from others in learning new adaptive behaviors for coping with stressful life situations. The end product of a psychological crisis can either be emotional growth or emotional equilibrium; from which new coping patterns can emerge. The outcome of these new adaptive behaviors can facilitate a higher level of emotional equilibrium, a state of balance. When an individual is faced with a crisis situation outside of his adaptive capacity tension and anxiety emerges. The goal in any crisis situation is to develop a problem solving strategy after identifying the problem to a level of emotional equilibrium that is sophisticated to what the person had before.

CHRISTIAN CRISIS INTERVENTION

·   Woman runs to the church

·   Assess the problem? Is there immediate danger?

·   Define the problem

·   Clarify the problem

·   No Criticism, show genuine concern, convey love, warmth and acceptance

·   Encourage emotional catharsis

·   Notify pastor, police and ambulance as appropriate..

·   Find out support network (are there children involved?)

·   Where is the nearest shelter or place of safety?

·   How much has the problem disrupted your life?

·   Ascertain the previous coping skills

·   Arrangements for follow-up as necessary

When preparing to leave:

· Always have some money put away in a safe place or with a friend or family member who you can trust.

· Remember to take your house keys, car keys.

· Birth certificates.

· Medications.

· Safety plans for the children: varies with the developmental age of the child.

· Give clear instructions to the school and day care about picking up the children.

· Provide physical signal outside the house for the children not to come in the house in the event there is violence at the time. Also a plan as to where the children will be dropped off until it is safe for them to return home. Remember to call the police at 911 or go to a designated place for help.

· In any abusive situation the goal is safety for the abused and her children.

· Safety plans for the pets: Pets are often the bait that the abuser will use to manipulate the woman for staying in the abusive relationship. Many abusers use verbal abuse of threats and cruelty to the woman's pets to prevent her from leaving.

·   Use of legal means: Knowing your legal rights

·   Call 911 or have a neighbor or friend call, state your name, address, and phone number. Identify whether your life is in danger.

CHAPTER 9
Spiritual Healing Process

HEALING AND WHOLENESS

a)   Acceptance of a new life (in Christ)
b)   Mind
c)   Emotions
d)   Physical
e)   Reconciliation
f)   Forgiveness
g)   "Letting-go"(of past)
h)   Restoration
i)   Resolution
j)   Spiritual therapy (i.e. communication of affirmations)
k)   Rebuilding of self-esteem

The question is "Wilt thou be made 'whole'? John 5:6

Healing and wholeness can only happen through dealing with the hurt and injury. To acknowledge that there is pain is to initiate the journey to wholeness. The mind being the seat of consciousness and being aware of the injury to her 'self' must now deal with the hurt and pain. This can be a battle for some abused women in that they find it difficult to understand that the journey is not going to be completed in one step. In fact it may take years for the whole process to be accomplished. The deep emotional scars that are confronted in the mind can distort the reality of joy, peace and happiness.

ACCEPTANCE OF A NEW LIFE: To accept Jesus, as your personal Savior is salvation in itself. Salvation a type of freedom from bondage and liberty to be the kind of person God had intended her to be. Every woman has potentials, talents, and gifts.

The acceptance of Jesus Christ will teach the abused woman how to accept Jesus' love and his forgiveness, to love, accept and forgive herself.

MIND. It is with the mind that we serve God and it is in the mind that the warfare takes place therefore when the woman is emotionally and psychologically abused her mind is in turmoil, fragmented and is in need of a complete therapeutic touch. Many times the abused woman's mind is confused and there is an array of negative thoughts that are circulating. The broken mind now attacks the self worth, confronts her with hopelessness and nothingness. The battle becomes fierce and stormy with ins, outs and bouts of depression that some abused women resort to alternatives such as drugs, and other codependent behaviors. This bereaved woman now needs the type of counselor that is in touch with her feelings and is sensitive enough to tap into her wounded spirit. A broken spirit and a wounded mind need the pouring in of God's love to heal the scars of abuse and put-downs. "A bruised reed shall he not break, and the smoking flax shall he not quench …" (Isaiah 42:3)

EMOTIONAL. The bruised reed represents the weakness of the abused woman who is broken physically, emotionally and spiritually but the Holy Spirit can mend the brokenness and revive hope. "A broken and a contrite spirit, O God thou wilt not despise (Psalm 51:17). This broken abused woman is troubled with her life and now looks to the only one that can truly protect her. The Christian counselor now has the task of presenting the love and compassion of Jesus Christ who understands brokenness. She needs an atmosphere that is conducive to **wholeness and healing.** Affirmations of scriptures and prayers should be utilized to heal the wounds and offering of hope.

PHYSICAL. Scars can be healed with time and the right kind of medicine but the emotional, and psychological scars of the mind can take a lifetime. It is a journey of undoing cruel negative thoughts while the abused woman needs to know that there is a balm in Gilead that heals all types of emotional and psychological scars, that is the power of Christian counseling. (Jeremiah 8:22).

RECONCILIATION. The abused woman needs to be friendly and accepting of herself regardless of her situation. Self-love is powerful and it is a sign of strength growth and maturity. This too is a journey that will be developed during the healing process. After all the woman has been verbally abused by name callings and the like over time which often she believes and think that she deserves, therefore; it is hard for her to suddenly love her self. The way to love and accept herself can be taught in light of the scriptures that she is fearfully and wonderfully made. Again, the notion of 'hope' needs to be communicated to her.

FORGIVENESS: Forgiveness is the epitome of the healing process. To not forgive is to hold unto the cancer that erodes the soul. It is easier for the abused woman to hate than to forgive she does have the right to hate or forgive. After all, her person, self-esteem and whole demeanor has been attacked and destroyed. Therefore one cannot lightly and frivolously resort to forgiveness without communicating to the woman the power and therapy that lies in the act of forgiveness. The abuser must be punished for his abusive behaviors but in counseling the Christian counselor must lead the counselee along the path of forgiveness to complete the healing journey. (Mark 11:25-26, Matthew 6:12,14,15).

To forgive some one that has violated your personage is to replace bitterness, anger and resentment with love. To forgive does not mean that you have suddenly forgotten the violence because the scars are there, but while in the process of forgiving you are basically acknowledging the hurt, while simultaneously relinquishing the denial, anger, and frustration. The abused woman is also hoping to welcome happiness, the ability to love and trust in other relationships. This journey is a process that completes over time. There maybe times when resentment tries to resurface with bouts of anger but the counselor will be able to facilitate the healing journey with many sessions until the counselee is spiritually and emotionally able to cope. Scriptural affirmations are very useful for comfort and reflections.

"LETTING GO": Letting-go" of the past is vital in the healing process..

"…but this one thing I do, forgetting those things which are behind, and reaching forth unto those things which are before" "I press toward the mark…" (Philippians 3:13-14). The scripture is saying that inspite of the fighting and the abusiveness the abused woman given the right kind of tools in counseling can concentrate on making a resolution in her mind to move to another level; that is discovering her new future. If the woman is determined to make that transition to the new level of thinking and living it can be done.

"I can do all things through Christ that strengtheneth me" (Philippians 4:13).

To not let go of the past is to deprive one's self from knowing what the future is about. To let go is to grow. The goal of the Christian counselor is to help the counselee make that positive transition.

Affirmation of the appropriate scripture should be part of the counseling session.

RESTORATION: "To restore is to give back something taken" (Webster's dictionary). The abused woman has been deprived of her mental and physical health and well being. This has been taken and scarred by the abuser but there is hope in that there is the notion of restoration, which comes through the journey, and process of healing. Relationships have been fractured, trust has been violated and nothing seems to make any sense but if the abused woman can conceive the validity of this scripture that "The Lord is my shepherd I shall not want. He maketh me to lie down in green pastures; He leadeth me beside still waters. He 'restoreth' my soul, He leadeth me in the paths of righteousness for his name's sake. Yea, though I walk through the valley of the shadow of death, I will fear no evil for thou art with me; thy rod and thy staff they comfort me" (Psalm 23: 1-4). This Psalm offers great security and reassurance. The mind can be restored to think pleasant thoughts and to welcome a brighter future. It is not impossible that the scarred mind can be restored over time during the healing journey. The Holy Spirit has the ability to totally heal and restore the mind. The abused woman can be restored to enjoy the goodness of life and be contented to accept the guidance of the Holy Spirit.

RESOLUTION: Webster's dictionary defines resolution as the act, or result of resolving something, a thing determined upon decision as to future actions. The abused woman during the journey to healing and wholeness can determine in her heart and mind to move on and refuse to live in the destructive past. One of her actions could be a decision not to return to the abusive relationship and be willing to try making it on her own given the appropriate tools and direction to start a new path. This might be frightening at first but with the help and support of those who care the decision to move on should be encouraged. The shepherd guides and will also provide.

SPIRITUAL THERAPY: This type of therapy is to bring one to an awareness of their own spirituality and consciousness of the inner person. Spiritual therapy is to bring healing and wholeness in light of the scriptures and biblical principles. It is therapeutic to know that there seems to be narrowing of the gap that once existed between psychology and theology. The American Psychological Association (APA) mandates that psychologists must take an informed view of religion as one of the significant dimensions of human differences or diversity or else make appropriate referrals. This is exciting and comforting that the gap is narrowing for the good of the counselee's. The American Psychiatrist Association's Committee on Religion and Psychiatry recommends that the religiosity of an individual be addressed in clinical practice. (Anderson, N; Zuehlke, T. E; & Zuehlke, J.S.). It is stated that the religious values have a crucial place in the ethical practice of mental health counseling is beginning to gain official recognition. A premise from professor Siang-Yang Tan the Fuller theological Seminary psychologist "A biblical approach to counseling… that explicitly utilizes Christian religious values or perspectives and interventions (prayer, use of

Scripture and relies on appropriate spiritual gifts and the power and ministry of the Holy Spirit makes unique contributions to counseling effectiveness, especially with religious, Christian client's."

The method utilized is to use Jesus Christ as the framework for healing. Jesus will be used as the healer for the wounded and abused body soul and spirit. Literature review has documented that true religion can bring about healing and integration of the whole person. To know Jesus Christ and the purpose of his dying was for the healing and salvation of man. "He was wounded for our transgressions he was bruised for our iniquities, the chastisement of our peace was upon him, and with his stripes we are healed". Isaiah 53:5

Jesus Christ is the expressed image of God and his entire teaching ministry was to the people. He showed, love, compassion and healing through his spoken word. He once called man to reason even though man was sinful and un-regenerated. "Come now, let us reason together, saith the Lord though your sins be as scarlet, they shall be as snow; though they be red as crimson, they shall be as wool" (Isaiah 1-18).

Jesus looks beyond all of human faults and sees the real need. He is interested in meeting needs through healing, forgiveness and restoration.

To deny Jesus Christ is to, deny the real existence of reality. The truth of the matter is that to be ignorant of Jesus is to be ignorant of one's eternal destiny.

The wounded need to know that the void that exist in the inner spirit is the quest for God. Man was made in his likeness and image therefore man does have his divine nature his genes if you will.

In the absence of a godly relationship there is turmoil, confusion and loneliness. Without a relationship with Jesus the healing and wholeness that man seek after is difficult to find. There is reassurance that "I will put none of these diseases upon thee; …for I am the Lord that healeth thee" (Exodus 15-26).

REBUILDING OF SELF-ESTEEM: The rebuilding of the self-esteem will be achieved through the insight of knowing the worth and potential of the whole person through affirmation of the scriptures. For example "I am a Son of God and I am valuable. "I am worth respect and honor." "I am a survivor and I can make it." "I can do all things through Christ that strengtheneth me." "I am fearfully and wonderfully made." "I am beautiful because I am made in the image of God." "No evil shall come nigh my dwelling." "I will cast all my cares upon him."

– Spiritual Healing Process –

PASTORAL COUNSELING

God
Creator
Provider
Sustainer
Deliverer

Through
Sacrificial Love
Provides

Jesus Christ
Salvation
Redemption
Justification
Regeneration

Natural Man
Rebellious
Disobedient
Sinful
Lost Identity
Degenerated
Confused Mind
Broken Relationships

Encounter with Christ

Actions
Repentance
Acceptance of Jesus Christ
Submisison
Renewed mind

Brings Healing

Results
Salvation
Acceptance
Sonship
Fellowship
Eternal Life

Norma Barnett 2003

Acceptance of Jesus Christ brings healing for the mind, body and soul. The Christian counselor will use biblical concepts as a paradigm for counseling – prayer, Bible reading, affirmation of scripture. The counselor will have a knowledge of Jesus Christ as the saviour of all and his purpose for humanity.

The Christian counselor will be knowledgeable of the nature of man and his relationship with Christ. Christian counselors will access discerning from the Spirit to facilitate the identification of the problem and lead the counselee to healing through Christ.

Behavior therapy

There are many strategies that are utilized for counseling and Behavior Therapy is a type of counseling strategy that is utilized. The concept of behavior therapy is that behaviors are learned and therefore can be unlearned. Researchers state that abusive behaviors are learned from significant others. The abuser possibly was also a victim of violence, which was utilized as a means of power and control.

For the purpose of this book the example of behavior therapy is being utilized. The goal of any behavior therapy is to get individuals to change and develop new adaptive behaviors and that the behaviors will be lasting. In the case of the abusive man his behaviors will change over time and be replaced with reasoning and dialogue instead of yelling and battering.

1. the goal of the counseling session is to help the abuser gain insight and increase his awareness of his abusiveness.
2. define the problem
3. the therapist will help the abuser design strategies on how to diffuse abusive negative behaviors

4.. design strategies on how to facilitate new and positive behaviors

5. offer praise and accomplishment for any effort to change

6. help the individual to make the paradigm shift.

As a counselor the best approach should be employed that will best meet the needs of the counselee. Both behavioral, spiritual and other therapies can work together in changing lives.

CHAPTER **10**

The Counselor

CHRISTIAN COUNSELING AND THE THERAPEUTIC PROCESS.

What is Counseling? The term counseling is defined in many ways by different authors depending on their frame of reference. According to (Pepinski, 1954) Counseling is a process involving an interaction between a counselor and a client in a private setting, with the purpose of helping the client change his or her behavior so that a satisfactory resolution of needs may be obtained. Although there are different definitions cited the basic outcome is the same that is helping some one to change. The Bible states, "in a multitude of counselors there is safety"(Proverbs 24:6).

According to (David Geldard) counseling can be defined as a one to one relationship between the counselor and the counselee. This relationship can be conducted face to face or sometimes by phone. Counseling can also be as a helping relationship where the counselor helps the counselee to change his or her behavior or look at what is happening in his or her life at this time. The counselor as a helper tries to assists the individual to understand his behaviors and to deal with internal or external behaviors.

Helpers can be informal such as friends, volunteers, relatives, church associates, pastors, laity, or professionals who are trained in the social, psychological, and counseling areas. The lay helpers are also called paraprofessionals. Helping another human being is basically a process of enabling that person to grow in the directions that person chooses, to solve problems, and to face crises (Bramer, L).

(Narramore C.M. 1976) states that a minister who does not place strong emphasis on counseling is only 'half a minister'. Why is counseling so important? Mainly, because it focuses on the needs of individuals. Jesus himself is a mighty counselor and has always met the needs of the people. He is always in touch with the feelings of their infirmities. "For we have not an high priest which cannot be touched with the feeling of our infirmities" (Hebrews 4:15).

Some of the basic skills used in counseling are listening, attending, perceiving, communication, exploration, problem solving, reframing, and clarification.

PROCESS FOR PASTOR /LAITY IN MEETING THE NEEDS OF THE COUNSELEE.

1.   Pastor as the counselor decides on what techniques he will implement in meeting the needs of the counselee. After the pastor has taken the initial assessment of gathering the facts of why the counselee comes to the session that will facilitate the proper counseling strategy to meet the counselee's needs. e.g. Christian counseling, Behavior Therapy.

2.   The pastor as a counselor should have knowledge of human behavior and be able to identify the different developmental stages and the tasks that each individual should master at that developmental level.

3.   Should be knowledgeable of different reading resources available. Eg. man and his relationship with man, the environment, and with God.

4.   Should counsel within a Christian context.

5.   Rely on the Holy Spirit for guidance and spiritual discernment

6.   Seek wisdom from above to know how to deal with different counselees and different behavioral situations.

7.   Know when to do referrals to the correct source so that the counselees needs can be met. This is the goal of counseling.

GOALS OF COUNSELING

According to (George, R.L.& Cristani, T. S). There are five major goals of counseling.

1.   **Facilitating behavior change** helping the counselee to live a more productive meaningful life. The goals set at this time should be specific and obtainable.

2.   The second major goal is **enhancing coping skill,** which help the individual to cope with new situations and new demands. The counselor helps the client acquire coping skills that will change and enhance his life.

3.   The third major goal is **promoting and decision making** where the counselee learns to make critical decisions and learns new problem solving skills. The client is

responsible for making his own decisions and for choosing alternatives. The counselor should not make decisions for the counselee. The client will learn to identify the consequences of the choices made. According to Reaves and Reaves (1965) "The primary objective in counseling is that of stimulating the individual to evaluate, make, accept and act upon the choice".

This will help promote growth and independence in the counselee to avoid prolonged dependency on a counselor.

4. The fourth major goal is **improvement of relationship** which is critical in an abusive relationship. We live in a social arena where we must have relationship with individuals daily. If individuals have not the proper social skills, and have low self-esteem, promoting defensive behaviors which affect their relationships, one can envision the difficulty that exists in maintaining healthy relationships. For this reason the ultimate goal of the counselor is to promote and facilitate healthier interpersonal relationship in the counselee's daily life.

5 The fifth and final goal is **facilitating client potential.** The task is for the counselor to help the client develop his or her personal

growth and to maximize personal effectiveness within the limitation of his environment. Also taking control over his own destiny. For example the client will take care of his mental heath, physical health, and learn how to overcome drug addiction. In the case of the abused woman she would be able to identify the abusive relationship, the triggers that would precipitate a violent episode and take the appropriate measures to protect her well being.

ASPECTS OF THE COUNSELING SESSION:

The counselor as a successful helper may use many approaches and strategies but the most effectiveness of any strategy is the building of trust during the sessions. Trust is developed during the first stage of the counseling session, which is called the **relationship phase.** The relationship phase is the development of rapport, trust, honesty, and empathy. The development of trust starts with the initial meeting of the counselor and the counselee at the interview. This is the first contact between the two people. The counselor must create a therapeutic climate that the counselee will be able to explore the problems and identify any underlying concerns as well as obvious concerns. The exploring skills will help the counselee clarify his or her needs and be able to make the appropriate actions of choice. During this initiation the goals and objectives must be mutually agreed upon to continue the counseling process. During the second phase of the counseling session **communication skills** are brought into play. The communication skills are both verbal and nonverbal. The verbal communication is what is verbalized or said by the counselee. It is important to pay attention to the feeling tone of the counselee when he or she verbalizes a statement.

Nonverbal communication is more powerful and often times communicate more than the spoken words. Nonverbal communications are exhibited through body language such as posture, gestures, eye contact, tone of voice, facial expressions, and the like. As a counselor you must pay attention to the inconsistencies of the verbal and nonverbal messages, while trying to increase the counselee's awareness of what is happening. Point out to the counselee that what is being verbalized is not congruence with the body language.

There must be mutual agreement for contract in helping the relationship, mutual acceptance of defined goals, planning and evaluations strategies, termination and follow up. Once the outcomes agreed upon by both parties have been met the termination of the helping process will be accomplished bringing closure. The hope is that the counselee would have gained self-reliance and self-confidence to maintain the new behaviors that have been learned to maximize his or her new lifestyle. This is the goal of counseling.

The third phase of the counseling session is critical in that **issues and values are being identified and clarified.** Issues such as intra-personal, inter-personal are important in that each individual behavior is based on their frame of reference. The counselor also brings to the counseling session his own values and issues which might be in conflict with the counselee. It is vital that the counselor is honest and open with the understanding that regardless of the difference in values the counselee must be respected and accepted unconditionally. The counseling session is not for the counselor but rather for the counselee that his or her needs can be met.

EFFECTIVE COUNSELORS

Effective counselors help the counselee to gain insight in his or her present situation during the relationship phase with the purpose of enabling the counselee to assume responsibility for themselves and make their own decisions. Counselors should not try to solve the problems but facilitate the counselee through identification, exploration, understanding, thereby taking the appropriate steps to bring about a behavior change. This can only be achieved through the effectiveness of a mutual relationship between counselor and counselee. The counselors skill in communication, understanding of the counselee's feelings, adequate problem solving methods, and the ability of the counselor to provide and utilize the appropriate strategy that best fit each individual counselee.

INTERPERSONAL SKILL COMPETENCIES

- Convey warmth, support, and empathy.
- In touch with their experiences and feelings
- Awareness of their own values and needs
- Awareness of their own limitations
- Develop warm relationships with other counselors
- Genuineness
- Accept personal responsibility for their own behaviors
- Set realistic goals
- Strive for excellence
- Accept constructive criticism

- Flexible not being rigid in their methodology
- Know when to refer clients to other counselors

QUALITIES AND TRAITS RECOMMENDED DURING COUNSELING

ATTENDING SKILLS: The counselor should give undivided attention to the counselee. The counselor cannot afford day dreaming, wandering eyes, impatience, or preoccupation and the like. The counselor must pay attention to facilitate a relationship.

ACTIVE LISTENING: Gary Collins, Christian Counseling (Page 43) states that listening is an active process that involves setting aside your own conflicts and biases to concentrate on what the counselee is communicating.

- Avoid subtle verbal or nonverbal expressions of disapproval or judgment about what is said.
- Using both your eyes and your ears to detect messages that come from the tone of voice, posture gestures, facial expressions and other nonverbal clues.
- Hearing not only what the counselee says, but noticing what is left out.

·   Waiting patiently through periods of silence or tears as the counselee summons enough courage to share something painful or pauses to collect his or her thoughts and regain composure.

·   Looking at the counselee as he or she speaks, but without either staring or letting your eyes wander.

·   Realizing that you can accept the counselee without condoning the actions, values, or beliefs. This is the concept of Unconditional Positive Regard where the person is always respected and accepted regardless of their behavior (Carl Rogers)

EMOTIONAL STABILITY: The counselor should be emotionally stable and be in touch with his or own feelings, biases and not bring them to the counseling session. The counseling session is not the place or time to ventilate biases, feelings, or personal concerns. The purpose of the counseling session is to give guidance, directions and facilitate behavior change in the counselee.

TRANSPARENCY OF SELF: Carl Rogers' concept of 'Congruence' means that the counselor must be genuinely honest, be complete integrated and whole. The counselor cannot be pretentious or tries to be someone else as this would abort the purpose of the counseling session. The counselor cannot wear a mask but rather be a real person with strengths and weaknesses who is relying on divine guidance. Recognizing that no one counselor has all the answers and that some sessions can be very difficult and need divine intervention. "In all thy ways acknowledge him, and he shall direct they paths"(Proverbs 3:6).

GENTLENESS: This is one of the fruit of the Holy Spirit and should be one of the character of the Christian counselor. Gentleness actually means kindness and showing kindness to the counselee will also facilitate a positive relationship.

IMPARTIALITY: The ability to counsel without bias being fair.

GOODNESS is also a fruit of the Holy Spirit, to demonstrate kindness.

NON-JUDGEMENTAL: The ability to counsel without judging or condemning the counselee. Not to form an opinion on values that are incongruent with your belief. Do not criticize but try to understand the counselee's frame of reference. "Judge not, that ye be not judged" (Matthew 7:1).

DISCREET: It is very important that the counselor be discreet and treat privileged information with great confidentiality. Information discussed during counseling session must not be used for gossiping or table talk. At the onset counselee's should be notified that all sessions are confidential except for information that may put themselves and others at risk which must be reported. (Prov. 20:19)

Professional Ethics

Ethics is conduct, morality, money and principles of right or wrong.

Information of the client is to be kept confidential. It is a privilege for someone to unveil themselves, so be careful how you handle written information. File in a secure locked place. Avoid using case material in presentations. For example, change names and conceal identifications.

- Avoid criticism of other counselors (pastors)
- Avoid touching the counselee. It could convey the wrong message except for a handshake.
- Avoid becoming emotionally involved.
- Be professional
- Pastor/counselor as a therapeutic helper
- Trusting relationship
- Accepting
- Open communication
- Warmth

- Genuineness
- Flexibility
- Sincerity
- Trustworthy
- Believe in individual
- Commitment
- Understanding of self
- Sharing
- Encouraging
- Promote forgiveness

Qualities of Christian counseling in meeting client needs

SPIRITUAL DIMENSION

1. **Spirituality:** Man is made up of body soul and spirit. The body is operated through the senses to cope with our world. The soul constitutes the mind and our perceptions while the spirit part of man is the entity that communicates with the supernatural being. The Christian counselor needs to be in touch with their own spirituality so that they can help understand the emptiness and thirst of a fragmented person who desires to be whole again. This is true of the abused woman who often times loses faith in her Christian beliefs

and the concept of God being there. The abused woman often times ask "how can this happen if there is a God why didn't he stop the abuse?"

2.	**Sensitivity to the Holy Spirit:** is highly recommended as many times the person that comes for counseling does not always present the real issue. This may be because they are afraid or ashamed, but the Holy spirit can detect and discern the truth of what is really happening on the inside of this fragmented person. Once the truth is revealed there can be positive help.

3.	**Prayerful life**: The Bible states "…that men ought always to pray and not to feint" (Luke 18:1). If the counselor has a prayerful life the guidance that is needed will be forth coming which will enhance the ability to help the counselee

4.	**Fasting and prayer:** are powerful tools that facilitate spiritual growth and causes the Christian counselor to be more effective in dealing with difficult situations.

5.	**God dependent:** means to be reliant on God for guidance.

6.	**Compassionate:** The counselor cannot counsel without compassion and being merciful. Jesus was moved with compassion,

(Mark 1:41) as he was concerned about the people's welfare. He always took the time to pay attention, even to little children.

7.   **Meditation:** The Christian counselor can take time to meditate examine his thoughts and then reflect on each individual. The Christian counselor can also reflect and evaluate his actions with possible measures to refine his counseling skills.

8.   **Discernment of spirit.**

KNOWLEDGE DIMENSIONS

1.   Study of the Word
2.   Knowledge of the doctrine
3.   Concepts of other doctrine
4.   Sound biblical Teaching
5.   Obedience to the Word
6.   Obedience to God's Will

UNDERSTANDING FAMILY ABUSE/ VIOLENCE

1.   Family dynamics
2.   Developmental cycle
3.   Interpersonal relationships
4.   Parental education/guidance
5.   Human sexuality

CHAPTER 11

Presentation of the Abused Woman

Presentation of the Abused Woman in the 21st Century was delivered on June 16th, 2001 in Edmonton Alberta sponsored by Canadian Apostolic Ministries (CAM) of which I am a newly elected member of the Board of Directors. The audience consisted of both genders, varied ages, men of the cloth, laity, Christians and non-Christians, which gave the audience an added dimension. The presentation was commenced with prayer for guidance and the right atmosphere to be conducive for deliverance and healing.

The whole objective of the "offering" of the topic was to raise an awareness of the reality of the issue and to have it discussed openly. The format of the presentation was that of participatory response from the audience, coupled with the viewing of a film entitled "One hit leads to another". This video was 15 minutes in duration but was profound and spoke volumes on the topic of "Abused Women" in our society.

As I watched the audience it was an emotionally charged atmosphere as participants openly cried while some were silent. Myself as the presenter openly participated in the emotions and expressed my concerns about the issue. There were other participants who took the risk, of being transparent in the audience and openly shared their story that greatly moved me.

The highlight of this whole presentation occurred when I was able to move under the unction of the Holy Spirit, put my arms around an abusee and as we both cried I was able to minister to her inner feelings. There were other participants that secretly came to me and expressed themselves, shared their story as we exchanged telephone numbers. As a result of this presentation and the visitation of the Holy Spirit one of the participants gave her life to the Lord on that Saturday, June 16th, 2001 and is now a member of one of the local churches.

This is the power of deliverance as the power is in the love. "The letter killeth but the spirit giveth life" (II Corinthians 3:6). From the "Abused

Woman" seminar an abused woman was set free from emotional pain. For this I am very grateful and feel committed to the task of promoting education against family violence. To God be the glory. The entire presentation lasted for one hour and three quarter.

The participant who was baptized requested the scriptural affirmations that I used. I readily gave her the scriptural affirmations as the power of life and death is in the tongue and as a man thinketh so is he (Proverbs 23:7). I coached her on how to affirm the Scriptures until they become a part of her spirit and instructed her to affirm them daily.

RECOMMENDATIONS FOR CHURCH PASTORS

The world and the church are full of hurting people and the church also has incidents of abuse in women that never really surface. But whether overt or covert the leaders need to be aware of the reality of wounded abused women and face the challenge of reaching out to them through the medium of prayer, fasting and counseling.

"In seminary, they never told us that so many people are needy", "They never warned us that a pastor might have to deal with mate beating, father-daughter incest, fear, confusion, threats of suicide, homosexuality, alcoholism, drug abuse, depression, anxiety, guilt, family problems …and a host of other societal maladies (Collins, Gary R. p. 15).

The concept of Counseling might be new, gigantic and fearful for the Church to deal with, but God has not given us the spirit of fear but of love and power and of a sound mind (2 Timothy 1: 7). Therefore the church leaders need not fear but be open to the Holy Spirit for guidance on how to deal with the abusive situation. They may enhance their studies by taking counseling courses through local community colleges, reading articles related to counseling, family dynamics, societal issues, and attend offerings at the local libraries that are often times free. They will broaden their own spiritual, and intellectual growth. In turn, this will enhance their leadership and ability to pastor God's people. Jesus Christ is a great Counselor and taught His disciples how to deal with issues of their day. Apostle Paul was very much in touch with people's feelings and documented that "We that are strong must bear the infirmities of the weak" (Romans 15:1).

"Counseling may seem like a waste of time but it is biblically mandated, and can be an effective, important, and necessary part of any ministry". The church should envision a halfway house or a recovery home where abused women can spend as much time as is needed to learn new skills for being reintroduced into society as well as restoration for the soul. In these houses people that are highly aware of the intricate issues surrounding abused women and their needs for spiritual deliverance will instruct, refer, guide, motivate and educate them on how to be independent, to improve their self-esteem, and to be successful in their spiritual and career endeavors.

CHAPTER 12
Tribute to Abused Women

"…Daughter be of good comfort; thy faith hath made thee whole and the woman was made whole from that hour" (Matthew 9:22).

Wholeness can only be therapeutically achieved through the touch of the master's hand. Abused women have both physical and emotional scars – wounds that can penetrate deep in the soul and viscera of each fabric of their personality. Damaged relationships and wounded emotions are a type of captivity locked into an ocean of negativity, drowning on hopelessness and abandonment, laced with fear. Not only physical and emotional abandonment but spiritual isolation.

Inspite of the cycle of despair there is **"HOPE"** (Psalms 42:11) "Why art thou cast down O my soul? And why art thou disquieted within me? "Hope thou in God" Hope for abused women who have been locked into the vicious cycle of pressure, fear, intimidation, tension, explosion, deceit, honey moon phenomena, deception and the like. Here is the moment of **"HOPE UNLOCKING THE DARKNESS"**, Jesus says in (Luke 4:18) "…heal the broken hearted, to preach deliverance to the captives and recovery of sight to the blind, to set at liberty them that are bruised". In other words for 'abused women" there is a way out. You choose to stay locked into the abusive cycle or to be liberated. Do you want to use a new set of keys? Do you have the strength to walk away not by your self but with the help of God? (Philippians 4:13) "I can do all things through Christ that strengtheneth me". You do not have to contend with the victimization you can unlock your own destiny, the prison door that confined, govern your life, and walk into the arms of God's freedom. There is a greater '**SHELTER**' than any physical shelter; there is a greater agency than any other agencies current. "God is my refuge and strength, a very present help in trouble" (Psalm 46:1)

I will acknowledge that "abused women" will experience some difficulty in letting go of the past feelings of fear, negative emotions that bound them for so long, but I come to challenge and declare them free from bondage and abuse if by faith they will give God a chance in their lives, asking for strength to forgive the abuser. "Forgetting those things, which are behind…" (Philippians 3:13).

If "abused women" continue to hold on to their past pain they will never experience the future gain. They must learn to let go so they can take in. It's like holding unto stale carbon dioxide that pollutes the respiratory system they need fresh oxygen to circulate in the emotional systems. Having experienced the old, they must now open up to experience the new. **"A new set of Keys"**. Open up and allow God to ingress in their spirit so they can feel and experience His divine flow of the Holy Spirit; it has the ingredients for their healing. With time caring and sharing every fractured emotional relationship will be healed through the process of healing and counseling. The church then can be an invaluable place for this type of healing and deliverance. It is deemed a safe institution that should not judge, or put down, but accept; love unconditionally, restoring "abused women "to a healthier stage of life.

FREEDOM

Appendices

APPENDIX A
FAMILY VIOLENCE IN CANADA: FACTS

·   Family violence and abuse affects all of us; no one is immune to violence.

·   Abuse occurs in all forms of relationships including parent-child, caregiver-client, adult child-parent, dating, gay and lesbian, marital and common-law and sibling.

·   Since the age of sixteen, 51% of Canadian women report having experienced at least one incident of physical or sexual violence.

·   Nearly three in ten Canadian women (29%) who have ever been married or lived in common-law relationship have been physically or sexually assaulted by a marital partner at some point during the relationship; 21% of these women were assaulted during pregnancy.

·   Of 22,000 victims of spousal violence reported to a sample of 179 Canadian police agencies in 1997, 88% (19,575) were female and 12% (2, 679) were male.

·   Children witnessed violence against their mothers in almost 40% of violent marriages; in many cases of children witnessing violence, the violence was so severe that the women feared for their lives (52%) and/or were injured (61%).

· Nearly one quarter of women (22%) who have experienced wife assault never told anyone about the abuse.

· Violent men are three times as likely as nonviolent men to have witnessed spousal violence in childhood, and women were raised in similar circumstances are twice as likely to be victims of spousal violence.

· Between 1978 and 1997, 1,485 females and 442 males were killed by their spouses in Canada.

· A total of 90,792 women and children were admitted to 413 shelters for battered women across Canada in 1997-1998.

· In 1996, children under 18 represented 22% of victims of assaults reported to a sample of 154 police agencies; children represented 60% of all victims of sexual assault and 18% of all victims of physical assault.

· Of sexual assaults by family members reported to police, girls were victimized in 79% of cases (1,662); while boys were victims in 21% of case (440).

·   The degree of risk of sexual abuse of persons with disabilities is "at least 150% of that for individuals of the same sex and similar age without disabilities.

·   In 1997, older adults accounted for 2% of victims of all violent crime reported to a sample of 179 police agencies; of these, 53% reported sustaining some type of injury.

·   Almost 25% of violent incidents against older persons reported to a sample of police in 1997 were perpetrated by family members; and while more older men were victimized by their adult children (41%) than by a spouse (28%), older women experience violence by adult children (40%) and spouses (40%) in equal proportions.

(National Clearinghouse on Family Violence).

APPENDIX B
FACTS ON NORTH WEST TERRITORY (NWT) WOMEN

NWT Status of Women Council February 2000
Note: In these fact sheets, "NWT" refers to the NWT after division; "NWT/Nunavut" will be used for statistics that are not broken down by territory.

GENERAL INFORMATION

· There were 19,210 females in the NWT in 1966 (census)
· Women are 48.4% of the NWT population aged 15 and over
· 13,610 females were age 15 or over

FAMILIES

· In 1996, single parent families represented 20% of families in NWT
· 79% of all NWT single parents are female
· In 1998 the NWT birthrate was 18 per 1000 population; the national rate was 11.
· NWT women have children at a younger age than Canadian women in general

· The birth rate for teen mothers in the NWT was almost three times the national rate. On average in the NWT there are 69 births for every 1000 teen women

· aged 15 to 19 each year.

CHILD DAY CARE

· In 1999 there were a total of 1152 licensed early childhood spaces in the NWT: 480 in centres, 382 in nursery schools, 90 in after school programs and 200 in family day homes.

· In 1995 there were 3245 NWT/ Nunavut women who were employed and had at least one child under age 6.

· Average day care fee for one child is approximately $600.00 to $700.00/month.

· There is no capital funding program to assist communities which have no suitable buildings in which to establish a day care centre

· Early Childhood Education training for day care workers is not consistently available.

POLITICS

· In 2000, 2 out of 19 members of the NWT Legislative Assembly are women (10.5%) and one woman is part of the Cabinet.

· In 1997, 37 out of 93 Metis Local board members were women (40%) and 3 out of 14 Metis Local Presidents were women (21%)

· 1 out of 30 Chiefs of band councils was a woman (3%)

· 114 out of 422 Hamlet/Band councilors (27%)

EDUCATION

· In 1999, 12.3% of NWT women over 15 had less than a grade 9 education

· Among NWT Aboriginal women, 25 % had less than a grade 9 but 41% had a high school diploma or other certificate or diploma.

INCOME AND EMPLOYMENT

· In 1999, 46% of all NWT workers were women

· A higher proportion of Aboriginal women (50%) were employed than Aboriginal men (46%)

·	The employment rate for Aboriginal women has increased almost 10% in the last 10 years, compared to a 2% among non-Aboriginal women.

·	85% of all non-Aboriginal women and 62% of all Aboriginal women in the NWT were part of the labor force in 1999.

·	In 1995 approximately 67% of NWT/ Nunavut women with children under age 6 were in the workforce and 55% were employed.

·	According to the 1996 census, 25% of senior management workers in the NWT were women

·	In 2000, women were the majority owners of 16% northern businesses.

·	The average income of NWT women in 1995 was $26,737 or 71% of the average income of NWT men (37,701).

·	35% of NWT women earned less than $20,000 and 14% earned $50,000 or more.

·	In 1995, the average employment income for NWT single parent families headed by women was $29,391, compared to $39,717 for male single parents and $68,123 for two-parent families.

WIFE ASSAULT

·   In Canada women were assaulted an average of 34 times before going to a shelter

·   From April 1999 to March 2000, 296 women and their 334 children used the NWT women's shelters. The rate of shelter use here is eight times the national rate.

·   The NWT has five family violence shelters.

·   In 1999, 436 cases of spousal assault by a male spouse were reported to the RCMP in the NWT.

NORTHERN SHELTER USE
APRIL 1999 - MARCH 2000

Location	Women Served	Children Served	Bed Nights
Yellowknife	85	77	1894
Inuvik	51	61	1708
Fort Smith	39	49	1456
Tuktoyaktuk	51	77	319
Hay River	70	70	1782
Total	296	334	7159

APPENDIX C
ALBERTA STATISTICS

The current attitudes are changing which are reflected in our laws:

1968 First time in Canada a spouse could gain a divorce re:cruelty.

1983 Police forces across Canada were instructed to lay charges of assault against offenders re: "domestic violence's" (Previously the victim was responsible).

1990 Alberta's Solicitor General reinforced the instruction that police should lay assault charges against wife abusers.

Past few decades: Canadians, Albertans have expressed increasing concern about wife abuse.

Alberta: First to have a **"WOMEN'S SHELTER" developed by VOLUNTEERS"**.

Currently many community groups have emerged to address and provide shelter and education to reduce family violence. Federal, Provincial and Territorial Ministers responsible for the Status of violence against women address the seriousness of this societal dilemma and in 1990 made a declaration outlining the impact of violence against women. Alberta Legislature and other officials are moving towards a safer environment, a society devoid of violence. As matter of fact one Alberta MLA expresses his concern stating that "No civilized society can allow some of its members to beat upon others". Indeed, violence against women is a crime and the offender should take full responsibility for his or her action. The Lake Louise Declaration on Violence Against Women May 1990 has also endorsed the inherent worth and dignity of women being violated through violence and victimization. One of the goals is to eliminate violence against women through prevention, public education, services and law enforcement. Goals can only be accomplished through community, church and government networking all their efforts to combat the forces of violence and save the family unit as intended.

The church should not be exempt from participating in addressing the societal maladies that affect all of us.

APPENDIX D
CANADA STATUS

1987 One in eight Canadian women cohabiting with a male partner experiences some form of abuse.

Studies conducted by University of Alberta and Calgary report similar studies.

1988 Over 4,923 women and over 6,002 children sought refuge in Alberta's women's emergency shelters and satellite shelters.

(These statistics do not include families that take refuge in hotels, motels, and other types of accommodation).

Statistics Canada report: An average of 100 women are murdered per year by their male partners.

Donald Sutton Canadian author and researcher, estimates that repeated severe violence occurs 1 in 14 marriages.

1989 Police responded to 5,451 incidents of spousal abuse. Of these 3,814 saw charges laid (70% charging rate).

89% of cases males were charged.

8% females were charged.

3% cases both parties, (female, male).

1998 Calendar year: The Alberta Department of Justice reported the following statistics:

Calgary Police Service responded to 1,894 reported cases of spousal assault, or ex-spouse.

Edmonton Police Service responded to 6, 525 cases of spousal assault.

RCMP responded to 2,246 cases of spousal assault in their areas.

APPENDIX E
DAILY AFFIRMATIONS

- I am fearfully and wonderfully made.
- I will not fear what man can do to me.
- God is my Helper and my counselor.
- God is my refuge and protector.
- God is my strength I will not fear weakness.
- I am strong and will be courageous.
- I refuse to stay bound and locked in.
- I will no longer hate myself.
- I will love myself.
- I am never alone because God is with me.
- I accept God's unconditional love.
- I am a woman designed by God.
- I will release my repressed anger
- I will forgive the abuser(s)
- I will not be afraid to reach out to others for fear of rejection

APPENDIX F
INSTRUMENTATION OF LOVE

Master, make me a channel of blessing
That I might bless others.
Make me an instrumentation of love,
That I might love others.
A flame of fire
That I might ignite others for Christ,
A wedge of righteousness to block sinful desires,
Lord, inhibit my fears and dispel doubt
That I might encircle a realm of faith.
Control my thoughts
That I might think pure as thou art
Embrace my love that my emotions
Will surround you
&
above all else – help me to love,
Love complete.
Norma Barnett

APPENDIX G
PRAYER OF ST. FRANCIS

Make me a channel of your peace
Where there is hatred, let me bring your love,
Where there is injury, your pardon Lord,
And where there is doubt, true faith in you.
Make me a channel of your peace.
Where there's despair in life, let me bring hope.
Where there is darkness only light,
And where there's sadness ever joy.
O Master, grant that I may never seek,
So much to be consoled as to console.
To be understood as to understand.
To be loved, as to love with all my soul.
Make me a channel of your peace.
It is in pardoning that we are pardoned.
In giving to all men that we receive,
And in dying that we're born to eternal life.
Sebastian Temple

APPENDIX H
HEALING FROM THE SCRIPTURES

"Ye are Clean through the Word"
St. John 15:3

Rejection   Marital Conflicts Bitterness   of Spirit
Isaiah49:16 Eph.5:21   Eph.4:31-32
Isaiah43:1
Jer.30:17

Physical Abuse   Loss of Spouse   V e r b a l Abuse
Psalm147:3 Isaiah54:5   Jer15:15-16
Psalm57:3   Psalm34:19-20   Psalm31:20
Isaiah54:17

Absence of Love   Mental and Emotional Abuse Loneliness
Jer.31:3   Isaiah61:3   Isaiah40:1
Isaiah43:1   Psalm30:3   Gen28:15
Psalm147:3 Matt.28:20
Jer31:13

Loss of Parent   Sexual Abuse   Loss   of Child/Children
Psalm68:5   Psalm147:3 IICorinthians1:3-4

Psalm27:10 Psalm107:20

Stress Fears Envy and Covetousness
IPeter5:7   Psalm91:4-6I C o r i n t h i a n s 1 2 : 7-
11
Matt.6:25   Psalm118:5-6   ITimothy6:6
Isaiah54:17
Isaiah41:13
Proverbs3:24
Psalm34:4

Jealousy   Sexual Sins Hatred
Psalm37:7   Hebrews2:18   Matthew5:44-45
Proverbs6:34   IThess.4:3-4P r o v e r b s 1 0 :
12
InferiorFeelings   Selfishness UnreleasedGuilt
IPeter2:9   Phil.2:4   1John1:9
Isaiah43:4   Heb10:17

Undefined Guilt   Loss of other Loved Ones
Unconfessed Sin
Psalm19:12 Mat5:4   Psalm41:4
Psalm103:12   Psalm32:5
Jer31:34   Psalm51:1
1John1:9

**Unforgiving Spirit   Low Self-Esteem
Financial Distress**

Mark11:25   Psalm34:2   Jer31:12
Matt6:14-15   Phil4:19
        Psalm34:10
        Luke6:38
        Isaiah41:17-18
        Psalm37:25

Uncontrollable Anger   **Inadequacies**
Psalm37:8   Phil4:13

Drugs   **Cults and the Accult**
(Prescribed & Illegal) Lev19:31
And Alcohol Abuse   2Cor7:1
Romans6:12-14   Titus2:11-14
1Cor10:13

Sexual Sins Depression Physical Sickness
Heb2:16   Psalm30:1-4 Psalm103:3
1Thes4:3-4 Isaiah43:3   Exodus15:26
Rom6:12,14 Phil4:7   3John2
1Cor10:13

Domineering   **Nagger**   **Inferior Feelings**
1Peter3:6   Prov.26:21 1Peter2:9
1Peter3:1,5 Prov.27:15 Isaiah43:4

Pride Unwise Spending Resentment
Prov.22:4   Isaiah55:2   Romans12:14

1Peter5:6   Matt.5:44
Phil.2:4
11Cor.10:17-18

Extremes in Dress   **Sexual Frustration**
Phil4:5   1Peter5:9
1Timothy2:9

APPENDIX I
TREATMENT PROGRAMS

There are a limited number of programs in Alberta directed at helping learn how to eliminate violent behavior.

Some counseling agencies and professionals in private practice offer individual counseling. Your nearest information and referral service may be able to direct you to these people.

Other agencies offer group therapy programs which focus on teaching non-destructive ways of expressing and managing anger and offer opportunities for examining ideas, attitude and behaviors which lead to violence. For more information contact the programs directly:

CALGARY

Calgary Counseling Centre
Family Violence Program
Suite 200, 940-6 Avenue S.W.
Calgary, AlbertaT2P 3T1

Ending the Cycle of Abuse
2003-16 Street S.E.
Calgary, AlbertaT2G 5B6
Phone: (403) 266-4111

Phone: (403) 265-4890   Fax: (403) 262-1743
Fax: (403) 265-8886   Org. - YWCA, Sheriff King
Org. - Calgary Counseling Centre   Family Support Centre
(M/F) (M/F)
Anger Management Program   Men's   Crisis Service
Elimination of Violence Group #265, 495-36 Street N.E.
Peter Lougheed Hospital Calgary, AlbertaT2A 6K3
Forensic Assessment and   Phone: (403) 299-9680
Outpatient Services   Fax: (403) 248-8851
Unit 37, 3500-26 Avenue N.E. Org. - Women's Emergency
Calgary, AlbertaT1Y 6J4 Shelter Association
Phone: (403) 291-8596   (M/F)
Fax:(403) 219-3521
Org. - Calgary Regional Health Authority
(M/F)
Probation Orientation Program
3rd Floor, 603-6 Avenue S.W.
Calgary, AlbertaT2P 0T3
Phone: (403) 297-6481
Fax: (403) 297-7750
Org. - Alberta Justice
(M/F)

CAMROSE
Changing Ways / Choices
c/o Messiah Lutheran Church
4810 - 50 Street

Camrose, AlbertaT4V 1P5
Phone: (780) 672-3444
(M/F)

EDMONTON
Changing Ways
Suite 201, 10426 - 81 Avenue
Edmonton, AlbertaT6E 1X5
Phone:(780) 439-4635
Fax:(780) 439-4635
Org. - Edmonton Family Violence
Treatment, Education and
Services
Research Centre
(M)
Family Violence Program
(M/F)

F.A.C.S.(Forensic Assessment
and Community Services)
8th Floor, 10242 - 105 Avenue
Edmonton, AlbertaT5J 3L5
Phone: (780) 428-0455
Fax:(780) 426-7272
Org. - Forensic Assessment
and Community
Research Centre (A service of the Alberta
Hospital Edmonton operated
under the Authority of the
9912 - 106 Street Provincial Mental Health
Edmonton, AlbertaT5K 1C5 Advisory Board)
(M/F)
Phone: (780) 423-2831

Fax: (780) 426-4918   Education for Abusive Men

Org. - The Family Centre Course
(M/F) Box 1796
          Edmonton, Alberta T5J 2P2

I.F.S.P. - Interpersonal and   Phone: (780) 497-4063

Family Skills Program   Org. - Grant MacEwan
8th Floor, 10242 - 105 Avenue C o m m u n i t y College (Life

Edmonton, AlbertaT6J 3L5   Management
Skills)

Phone: (780) 424-1747   (M)

Fax: (780) 497-7639

Org. - Forensic Assessment and
Community Services
(A service of the Alberta Hospital
Edmonton operated under the
Authority of the Provincial Mental
Health Advisory Board)
(M)

GRANDE PRAIRIE

Renaissance
9909 - 112 Avenue
Grande Prairie, Alberta
T8V 1V5
Phone: (780) 523-0373
Fax: (780) 538-4931

Org. - John Howard Society
(M)

LEDUC

H.E.A.L. - Help End Abuse in Leduc
1 Alexandra Park
Leduc, AlbertaT9E 4C4
Phone: (780) 980-7155
Fax: (780) 980-7127
Org. - Help End Abuse in Leduc
Service
(M/F)

LLOYDMINSTER

New Perspectives
Ltd.
P.O. Box 1523
Lloydminster, AlbertaS9V 1K5
Phone: (780) 875-0966
Fax: (780) 875-0609
Org. - Lloydminster Interval House
(M)

STONY PLAIN

Turning Point
9601 - 44 Avenue

LETHBRIDGE

Family Life Intervention Project
1107 - 2A Avenue North
Lethbridge, AlbertaT1H 0E6
Phone: (403) 327-5724
Fax: (403) 329-4924
Org. - Lethbridge Family
(M/F)

RED DEER

Jim Freeman Psychotherapist
Main Floor, 4805 - 48 Avenue
Red Deer, AlbertaT4N 3T2
Phone: (403) 343-9200
Org. - Jim Freeman Psychotherapist Ltd
(M)

WHITECOURT

New Start for Men Involved in Family Violence

Stony Plain, AlbertaT7Z 1W9   Box 509
Phone: (780) 963-7112   Whitecourt,   AlbertaT7S 1N6
Org. - RCMP/Victim Services Unit   Org.   -
Family and Community
(M)   Support Services
         (M)

BONNYVILLE
A Better Way Men's Group
Bag 1006
Bonnyville, AlbertaT9N 2J7
Phone: (780) 826-2120
Fax: (780) 4806
Org. - Bonnyville and District
Family and Community
Support Services
(M)

M/F = Male/Female

References

Aguilera, Donna C. & Messick, Janice M. (1982b). Crisis Intervention: Therapy For Psychosocial Emergencies. A Plume Book.

Alberta Family Social Services, (1991).

Alberta Family and Social Services. Breaking the Pattern: How Alberta Communities Can Help.

American Association of Counsclors and Prison Chaplain.

Anderson, Neil T.; Zuehlke, Terry E.; Zuehlke, Julianne S. Christ Centered Therapy The Practical Integration of Theology and Psychology. Zondervan Publishing House Grand Rapids, Michigan.

Armitage, Ronda. (1999). Family Violence. Raintree Steck-Vaughn Publishers.

Blackwell, Judith, & Jones-Farrow, Hilary (1990). One Hit Leads to Another: A *Study Guide*. National Film Board of Canada.

Brammer, Lawerence M. (1979). The Helping Relationship: Process And Skills. Prentice-Hall, Inc.

Brewster, Susan. (1997). To Be An Anchor In The Storm: A Guide for Families and Friends of Abused Women. Ballantine Books.

Clinebell, Howard. (1984). Basic Types of Pastoral Care & Counseling: Resources For The Ministry Of Healing and Growth (Revised and Enlarged). Abingdon Press.

Collins, Gary R. (1988). Christian Counseling: A Comprehensive Guide. Word Publishing.

Davies, Laura. (1991). Allies in Healing: When the Person You Love Was Sexually Abused As A Child. Harper Perennial.

Davis, Laura. (1990). The Courage To Heal Workbook: For Adult Survivors of Child Sexual Abuse. Harper & Row, Publishers.

Duffy, Ann & Momirow, Julianne. (1997). Family Violence: A Canadian Introduction. James Lorimer & Company, Publishers.

Dutton, Donald G. (1995). The Batterer: A Psychological Profile. BasicBooks.

Fawcett, Cheryl. (2000). Understanding People: Ministry To All Stages Of Life Evangelical Training Association.

Geldard, David. (1998). Basic Personal Counselling: A Training Manual for Counsellors. Prentice Hall.

George, Rickey L. (1981). Theory, Methods, & processes of Counseling & Psychotherapy. Prentice-Hall, Inc.

Hart, Archibald D., et al. (1992). Mastering Pastoral Counseling. Multnomah Press.

Health Canada, 1(994). Canada's Treatment Program For Men who Abuse Their Partners. Health Canada.

Hong, Maria. (1997). Family Abuse: A National Epidemic. Enslow Publishers, Inc.

Hulme, William E. (1981). Pastoral Care and Counseling. Augsburg Publishing House.

Heitritter, Lynn & Vought, Jeanette. (1989). Helping Victims of Sexual Abuse: A Sensitive, Biblical Guide for Counselors, Victims and Families. Bethany House Publishers.

James, Joan. (979). Make me Whole: An In-depth Study through the Scriptures On Inner Healing and Wholeness. Joan James Ministries.

Jantz, Gregory L. (1995). Healing The Scars of Emotional Abuse. Fleming H. Revell.

Jayne, Pamela. (2000). Ditch That Jerk: Dealing With Men Who Control And Hurt Women. Hunter House

King James Bible

Kritsberg, Wayne. (1992). The Invisible Wound: A New Approach to Healing Childhood Sexual Abuse. Bantam Book.

Lee, Valerie Lynch. (1990). Dysfunctional Families. The Rourke Corporation, Inc.

Lerner, Harriet G. (1989). The Dance of Anger: A Woman's Guide to Changing The Patterns of Intimate Relationships. Perennial Library.

Marks, Jane. (1976). A Guide to Counseling and Therapy Without A Hassle. Julian Messner.

Meyer, Joyce. (1965). Beauty for Ashes: Receiving Emotional Healing. Harrison House.

Morris, Bill M. (1993). The Complete Handbook For Recovery Ministry in The Church: A Practical Guide to Establishing Recovery Support Groups Within Your Church. Thomas Nelson Publishers.

McDowell, Josh & Hostetler, Bob. (1996). Handbook on Counseling Youth: A Comprehensive Guide for Equipping Youth Workers, Pastors, Teachers, Parents. Word Publishing.

Myers, David G., Psychology third edition Hope College Holland, Michigan Worth Publishers Inc. copyright 1986, 1989, 1992.

Narramore, Clyde M. (1976). The Psychology of Counseling: Professional Techniques for Pastors, Teachers, Youth Leaders, and all Who Are Engaged In The Incomparable Art of Counseling. Zondervan Publishing House.

Oates, Wayne E. (1974). Pastoral Counseling. The Westminster Press.

One Hit Leads to Another. Videocassette. Dir. Hilary-Farrow, Friday Street Productions, 1990. 15 min.

Office For The Prevention Of Family Violence. (1991). Breaking The Pattern: Understanding Wife Abuse. Edmonton, Allberta.

Rench, Janice E. (1992). Family Violence: How to recognize And Survive it. Lerner Publications Company.

Roesch, Ronald et. al [Editors] (1990). Family Violence: Perspectives on Treatment, Research, and Policy. British Columbia Institute on Family Violence.

Shebib, Bob. (1997). Counselling Skills. Ministry of Education Skills and Training, British Columbia.

Solomon, Charles R. (1977). Counseling With the Mind of Christ: The Dynamics of Spirituotherapy. Power Books.

Swisher, Karin, L. [et al]. (1994). Violence Against Women. Greehaven Press, Inc.

Wright, Norman H. (1985). Crisis Counseling: Helping People in Crisis and Stress. Here's Life Publishers.

Zimbardo, Philip G. and Weber, Ann L. Psychology second edition, Addison Wesley Longman, Inc. 1997.

About the Author

Dr. Norma Barnett is the Dean of Academics for Grace International Bible College in Edmonton, Alberta. Also Adjunct Professor of IAUGT College of Christian Counseling Dayton Ohio. Dr Norma Barnett has a Bachelor's degree in nursing, an Education Diploma in Adult education, a Bachelors and Master's degree in Christian Counseling and

Christian education She graduated with Summa-Cum-laude in Christian Counseling and has gained the certification of Certified Psychotherapist and Counselor with the E.O.P.C of America. As a devoted educator, speaker, counselor, writer, and nurse she has traveled and written many articles regarding the human experience from secular, as well as religious perspectives. She also facilitates the Women's Group at RTAC and runs a Women's Book club.

She resides in Edmonton Alberta and co-pastors with her husband. Not only does Dr Barnett speak about abuse but has counseled many abused women. She writes not to impress but to create awareness through education and enlightment of abused women of today. By doing this she hopes that some lives will be transformed through the power of the WORD of God.

www.ingramcontent.com/pod-product-compliance
Lightning Source LLC
Chambersburg PA
CBHW022202050726
47590CB00002B/609